Queer in AI Workshop (QueerInAI 2025)

Albuquerque, New Mexico, USA
4 May 2025

ISBN: 979-8-3313-1927-4

Printed from e-media with permission by:

Curran Associates, Inc.
57 Morehouse Lane
Red Hook, NY 12571

Some format issues inherent in the e-media version may also appear in this print version.

Association for Computational Linguistics
209 N. Eighth Street
Stroudsburg, Pennsylvania 18360

Phone: 1-570-476-8006
Fax: 1-570-476-0860

acl@aclweb.org

Additional copies of this publication are available from:

Curran Associates, Inc.
57 Morehouse Lane
Red Hook, NY 12571 USA
Phone: 845-758-0400
Fax: 845-758-2633
Email: curran@proceedings.com
Web: www.proceedings.com

QueerInAI 2025

Queer in AI Workshop

Proceedings of the Queer in AI Workshop

May 4, 2025

Introduction

We are excited to welcome you to the Queer in AI 2025 Workshop, co-located with NAACL 2025. The workshop is scheduled for May 4, 2025. Queer in AI provides a platform to discuss and present research that captures queer and gender-diverse perspectives in natural language processing (NLP), artificial intelligence (AI), and linguistics.
NLP and AI technologies pose risks to marginalized communities such as the queer community, especially when developed without participation from stakeholders of these communities. Hence, it is crucial to make sure that queer researchers are included in the study, development, evaluation, and broader discourse around NLP technologies. This workshop creates a dedicated space in conferences for queer scientists to discuss and network.
This workshop brings together researchers and practitioners, and advocates for working at the intersection of queerness and AI. It raises awareness of research and advocacy on how NLP and AI systems impact queer people and queer experiences in the NLP community. It also offers queer scientists a venue to disseminate and present their research.
This year, the workshop accepted 5 archival submissions and 3 non-archival submissions with topics spanning from hate speech detection, queer bias identification in large language models, and perspectives on queer cultures and neopronouns.

About Queer in AI:

Queer in AI is an active advocacy organization. Queer in AI was established by queer scientists in AI with the mission to make the AI community a safer and more inclusive place that welcomes, supports, and values LGBTQIA+ people. We build a visible community of queer and allied AI scientists through conference workshops and poster sessions, social meetups, mentoring programs, and numerous other initiatives.
We have been organizing this workshop as an affinity workshop of ACL since 2019. Because of a recent surge in Queer NLP and AI research, we are hosting the first archival Queer in AI workshop this year.

Acknowledgments:

This workshop would not be possible without the tireless work of queer rights activists who have paved the way for LGBTQIA+ visibility and inclusion in academic and professional spaces. We stand on the shoulders of those who have fought for recognition, respect, and equal rights for queer individuals throughout history, particularly transgender, non-binary, and BIPOC members of our community.
We extend our deepest gratitude to our dedicated volunteers who have contributed countless hours to organizing this workshop and growing the Queer in AI community. Their passion and commitment to creating inclusive spaces in AI are what make initiatives like this possible.
We are further indebted to our program committee members and reviewers who carefully evaluated submissions and provided thoughtful feedback to authors. Their expertise and dedication have been instrumental in curating a program that represents diverse queer perspectives in AI research. Finally, we would like to express our appreciation to all the authors who shared their work with us and all attendees who are participating in this dialogue, both at this workshop and in our prior affinity workshops.

Organizing Committee

Workshop Chairs

A Pranav, Data Science Group, University of Hamburg, Germany
Anne Lauscher, Data Science Group, University of Hamburg, Germany
Alissa Valentine, Mount Sinai, NYC, USA
Shaily Bhatt, Carnegie Mellon University, USA
Sabine Weber, University of Bamberg, Germany
Yanan Long, University of Chicago, USA
Arjun Subramonian, University of California, Los Angeles, USA
Amanda Bertsch, Carnegie Mellon University, USA
Ankush Gupta, IIIT Delhi, India

Core Organizers

Maria Ryskina, Carnegie Mellon University, USA
Shane Storks, University of Michigan, USA
Andrea Sipos, University of Michigan, USA
Juan Vasquez, University of Colorado, Boulder, USA
Anaelia Ovalle, University of California, Los Angeles, USA
Tao Long, Columbia University, USA
Vagrant Gautam, University of Saarland, Germany
Eddie Ungless, Google NYC, USA
Raj Korpan, City University, NYC, USA
Nathan Dennler, University of California, Los Angeles, USA
Martin Mundt, University of Bremen, Germany
Carter Buckner, University of Arkansas, USA
Claas Voelcker, University of Toronto, Canada
Danica Sutherland, University of British Columbia, Canada
Sharvani Jha, Microsoft, USA
Maria Leonor Pacheco, University of Colorado Boulder, USA
Luca Soldaini, Allen Institute for Artificial Intelligence, USA

Program Committee

Reviewers

Connor Baumler, University of Maryland, College Park, United States
Daniel Beck, Royal Melbourne Institute of Technology, Australia
Laura Carter, University of California, Berkeley, United States
Daryna Dementieva, Technische Universitat Munchen, Germany
Hannah Devinney, Linkoping University, Sweden
Jasleen Dhillon, University of Texas at Austin, United States
Vagrant Gautam, Saarland University, Germany
Coleman Haley, University of Edinburgh, United Kingdom
Cipriano Hdz, CIMAT, Mexico
Carolin Holtermann, Universitat Hamburg, Germany
Filip Miletic, University of Stuttgart, Germany
Sachita Nishal, Northwestern University, United States
Mohan Raj, Monash University, Malaysia Campus, Malaysia
Preethi Seshadri, University of California, Irvine, United States
Pushpdeep Singh, Tata Consultancy Services Limited, India
Shane Storks, University of Michigan, United States
Eshaan Tanwar, Indian Institute of Technology, Delhi, India
Jocelyn Wong, McGill University, Canada
Sierra Wyllie, University of Toronto, Canada

Table of Contents

Studying the Representation of the LGBTQ+ Community in RuPaul's Drag Race with LLM-Based Topic Modeling

Mika Hämäläinen
Metropolia University of Applied Sciences
Helsinki, Finland
firstname.lastname@metropolia.fi

Abstract

This study investigates the representation of LGBTQ+ community in the widely acclaimed reality television series RuPaul's Drag Race through a novel application of large language model (LLM)-based topic modeling. By analyzing subtitles from seasons 1 to 16, the research identifies a spectrum of topics ranging from empowering themes, such as self-expression through drag, community support and positive body image, to challenges faced by the LGBTQ+ community, including homophobia, HIV and mental health. Employing an LLM allowed for nuanced exploration of these themes, overcoming the limitations of traditional word-based topic modeling.

1 Introduction

The representation of LGBTQ+ identities in mass media is an important area of research to gain a better understanding on what kind of an image of the LGBTQ+ community is broadcast to the public. Media representations contribute significantly to the shaping of public perceptions (McCombs, 2002) and they influence on societal attitudes towards marginalized communities (see German 2017).

Within this context, RuPaul's Drag Race (RPDR)[1] has emerged as a prominent cultural artifact, offering a platform that foregrounds the art of drag and simultaneously engages with themes of gender, sexuality and queer culture (see Chan 2024). The series, which debuted in 2009, has garnered widespread acclaim and critical attention[2], becoming a touchstone for LGBTQ+ representation in mainstream entertainment.

Media and television studies have long studied the role of popular culture in reflecting and shaping societal norms and ideologies (Calvert et al., 2007). Television, as a mass medium, occupies a unique position in the cultural landscape, blending entertainment with implicit and explicit narratives about minority identities (Greenberg et al., 2002). Scholars have argued that television serves as both a mirror and a mold that offers audiences representations which both reflect their lived realities and influence their perceptions of the world (Ott and Mack, 2020). For this reason, it is important to study what kind of a picture of the LGBTQ+ RPDR paints, especially since it is one of the few widespread LGBTQ+ shows that is broadcast globally.

Furthermore, television studies have emphasized the interplay between audience reception and media production in how viewers actively interpret and negotiate the meanings embedded within televised texts (Jensen, 2002). These interpretations are shaped by cultural, historical and personal contexts, and thus they create a complex feedback loop between creators and consumers (see Hagen and Wasko 2000).

Recent advances in large language models (LLMS) provide new opportunities for analyzing large-scale textual data, which makes more detailed topic modeling possible as we no longer need to rely on word-level methods that were in fashion before LLMs. Topic modeling with large language models (LLMs) has emerged as a powerful tool for exploring thematic structures in text corpora (Pham et al., 2023; Kapoor et al., 2024; Invernici et al., 2024).

This study employs LLM-based topic modeling to analyze the representation of the LGBTQ+ community in RuPaul's Drag Race subtitles from seasons 1-16. By analyzing the transcripts of the show, we aim to see how it reflects and represents the LGBTQ+ community. This method helps us explore narrative and in-group attitudes portrayed in the show. Our goal is to contribute to conversations about how media portrays LGBTQ+ identities and

[1] A show produced by World of Wonder

[2] https://www.televisionacademy.com/shows/rupauls-drag-race

Proceedings of the Queer in AI Workshop, pages 1–5

to show how our method can help us understand these representations better.

2 Related work

RPDR is no stranger to scientific study. In this section, we will go through some of the recent body of work that has studied the show.

Edgar (2011) explores how the show frames drag performance through normalization, reinforcing stereotypical ideals of femininity while simultaneously illustrating the complexities of gender as a performative construct. By examining the experiences of key contestants, Edgar highlights how drag performance is judged not only by skill but by adherence to specific gendered expectations, such as natural beauty and the seamlessness of femininity. While the show borrows successful elements from other reality television formats to engage mainstream audiences, this normalization risks reducing drag to entertainment, sidelining its potential to subvert rigid gender binaries.

In the analysis of RuPaul's Drag Race (RPDR) by Brennan (2017), the author explores the interplay of authenticity, competition and consumption within the show, arguing that these dimensions both reflect and complicate the format of reality television. The study examines how authenticity is negotiated through drag queens' performances, revealing tensions between personal identity and constructed personas, while competition emphasizes individuality in a space shaped by neoliberal values and historical marginalization. Additionally, the author critiques the show's commercial underpinnings the highlight the role of branding and consumerism in shaping perceptions of drag culture.

In their article, Strings and Bui (2014) analyze the interplay of race and gender in the third season of RPDR. They argue that while the show challenges traditional notions of gender through drag performance, it enforces rigid racial authenticity, particularly for African American contestants. This duality allows gender to be fluid and performative, while race is treated as fixed and essential, leading to racial stereotyping and tensions among contestants. The authors highlight how these dynamics reflect broader societal patterns, where racial identities are commodified and constrained even within ostensibly progressive queer spaces.

Goldmark (2015) examines the complex interplay between reality television, queer identity and neoliberal ideals through the lens of the show's first season. The analysis critiques how RPDR employs narratives of transformation and success, tying them to aspirational themes of the American Dream. While the show celebrates diversity and individuality, the study highlights the underlying contradictions, particularly its reliance on cultural and linguistic hierarchies that privilege English and U.S. norms. The article also interrogates racial and economic disparities, showcasing how contestants like BeBe Zahara Benet and Nina Flowers symbolize both the potential and limitations of inclusion, complicating the program's portrayal of upward mobility and integration into an idealized U.S. nation.

3 Data

We use the subtitles of RuPaul's Drag Race for seasons 1 to 16 that are available on OpenSubtitles[3]. The seasons vary in length. The shortest season is the first season with only 9 episodes and the longest season is the 13th season with 17 episodes. A typical length of a season is 14 episodes. The corpus size for each episode can be seen in Table 1.

Season	Tokens	Season	Tokens
1	78k	9	104k
2	101k	10	172k
3	129k	11	153k
4	119k	12	165k
5	114k	13	199k
6	103k	14	182k
7	94k	15	155k
8	104k	16	179k

Table 1: Size of each season in tokens

The seasons extend from the first season released in 2009 to the 16th season released in 2024. Season 17 was excluded as it was still not fully released during this study. The judges have changed over the years and some queens have been featured in multiple seasons. The only judge who has appeared in every season is RuPaul himself.

The subtitle files were cleaned from timestamps and only text was retained. Some of the subtitle files were not encoded in Unicode format, which led to some encoding errors. These erroneous characters including some invisible Unicode characters

[3]https://www.opensubtitles.org/en/ssearch/sublanguageid-eng/idmovie-171453

The main LGBTQ+ conversation topics in these subtitles from RuPaul's Drag Race, focusing on Adore Delano's statements, are:

1. **Drag Identity and Performance:** This is central, encompassing Adore's stage name (Adore Delano, its meanings, and the humor around it), the contrast between their drag persona and their birth name (Danny), and the creation of catchphrases and overall performance style. The discussion of "wearing people's stories" through thrift store finds also speaks to the performative and expressive nature of drag.

2. **Family Acceptance and Support:** Adore discusses their relationship with their mother, highlighting a complex dynamic of love, criticism, and ultimately, support. This touches on common themes of family acceptance within the LGBTQ+ community. The mother's overbearing nature is portrayed humorously, but the underlying love is evident.

3. **Gender Expression and Identity:** The statement "I'm not a boy. So rude" directly addresses gender identity and the rejection of gender norms. The discussion of their natural pink hair and the frustration with pageant queens not understanding it speaks to the broader theme of self-expression and challenging beauty standards.

4. **Queer Community and Influences:** Adore mentions Alaska as their favorite queen, indicating a connection to and appreciation for other members of the LGBTQ+ community and the influence they have.

While there's humor and self-deprecation throughout, these subtitles reveal key themes relevant to LGBTQ+ experiences, focusing on self-discovery, family dynamics, the performance of identity, and community.,

Table 2: An example output from the LLM

were removed. This did not affect the textual content of the subtitles as they were in English and all English alphabets were encoded consistently across the files. Some of the subtitles included HTML tags such as <*i*> and <*b*>, these tags along with their possible attributes were deleted as well.

4 LLM-based topic modeling

We use Gemini 1.5 Flash (Georgiev et al., 2024) LLM to extract a list of LGBTQ+ related topics for each episode of each season. This is simply done by prompting the model through the API. We use the prompt template shown in Table 3 populated for each episode.

For the following subtitles from RuPaul's Drag Race, give a list of the main LGBTQ+ conversation topics.

Subtitles:

<Subtitle data>

Table 3: Prompt template used for extracting the topics

The prompt resulted in an analysis of the main LGBTQ+ topics discussed in the episode (see an example in Table 2). Every analysis has a list of topics indicated by a bolded topic title such as ***Coming out and self-expression:*** or ***Body image and eating disorders:***. Each title is followed by a further analysis of the topic. We sampled 5 LLM produced analyses randomly and compared the topics to what was discussed in the episodes. We found the LLM results to be of sufficient quality.

Using the topic titles, we separate each topic along with its description into different strings for each episode. We remove all text in the LLM answers that is not part of a topic description. This way, each episode is now described by a list of topic strings indicating the topic and description.

We use *text-embedding-004* model from Google Gemini API[4] to produce topic embeddings for each topic string. These topic embeddings are used to cluster the topics together with HDBSCAN algorithm (Campello et al., 2013) using UralicNLP Python library (Hämäläinen, 2019).

HDBSCAN does not require a fixed number of clusters, but it will find an optimal number of clusters on its own. We tested with several parameter values for minimum cluster size and found that 10 resulted in a good number of clusters that was still manageable to go through manually.

The algorithm found 43 cluster, which we further combined manually given that several clusters had similar topics but described using different wordings. The titles were often very similar if not identical, but the semantic contents of the descriptions were different enough for the clusters not being merged. We also tried affinity propagation clustering (Frey and Dueck, 2007), but didn't find it producing any better results, for this reason we proceeded to manual merging.

We removed a few topic clusters altogether because they did not deal with LGBTQ+, but were

[4]https://cloud.google.com/vertex-ai/generative-ai/docs/model-reference/text-embeddings-api

Topic	Occurrences	Topic	Occurrences
Ageism within the LGBTQ+ community	21	Drag as a form of self-expression and artistry	187
Mental health and resilience	54	Intersectionality (race and class)	27
Sisterhood and community	29	Gender expression and identity	60
Internalized homophobia and self-acceptance	77	Relationships and intimacy	60
LGBTQ+ community and representation	219	Negative body image and beauty standards	65
Representation and Visibility	86	Coming out and self-acceptance	159
The importance of community and family support	100	Positive body image and self-love	129
HIV/AIDS awareness and activism	11	Homophobia and discrimination	45

Table 4: Topic clusters and how often cluster topics appeared in the analyses

rather about the competition itself such as judging, winning and elimination. We also removed clusters related to humor because they were not LGBTQ+ related.

5 Results

The results of the clustering can be seen in Table 4. The topics listed in the table represent the topic clusters and the occurrences indicate how many times the topic was found the LLM analyses for the all the seasons.

The most commonly discussed themes were *LGBTQ+ community and representation*, which refers to being a representative of the LGBTQ+ community, *Drag as a form of self-expression and artistry*, *Coming out and self-acceptance*, *Positive body image and self-love* and *The importance of community and family support*. All in all, the most common themes are either empowering or can be seen as a growth story.

Although not in the list of the most common topics, RPDR also frequently visits negative themes that are typically seen as problematic for LGBTQ+ people such as *Mental health and resilience*, *Internalized homophobia and self-acceptance*, *HIV/AIDS awareness and activism*, *Negative body image and beauty standards* (including body dysmorphia) and *Homophobia and discrimination*. An additional negative topic that is perhaps not as stereotypically seen as an LGBTQ+ problem is *Ageism within the LGBTQ+ community*.

Some of the more positive and less frequent topics include *Sisterhood and community*, *Representation and Visibility*, which means representation of oneself and visibility as a public figure, *Intersectionality (race and class)*, *Gender expression and identity* and *Relationships and intimacy*.

6 Conclusions

Much of the prior work in research on RPDR has taken a rather critical and negative view on the show as evidenced in the related work section. However, if we look at the LGBTQ+ topic clusters found by our method, a different narrative can be perceived. A narrative of hope. Many of the topics are empowering such as how one can use drag to express themselves or how one is representative of a bigger LGBTQ+ community, i.e. one is not alone.

One can perceive hope through the difficult themes such as coming out and it ultimately leading to self-acceptance. And regardless of the bad thing such as homophobia (internalized or externalized) or the unrealistic beauty standards set by the society, one can still overcome them.

Our intention is not to invalidate any of the existing and more critical research. Our study simply revealed another side of the show. Despite of the problems the show has, our NLP approach has shown that the show serves an important puprose as a beacon of hope for LGBTQ+ people and, by discussing difficult themes that many of us queer people can relate to, the show delivers a message to their LGBTQ+ audience that they are not alone with their problems.

In the future, it would be interesting to study how the topics have evolved throughout the series from one season to another. Also, RPDR has been adapted to many other regions and languages. It would also be interesting to study what kind of topics exist in those shows and how comparable they are to the main series.

7 Limitations

When analyzing large amounts of textual data, no method comes without limitations. We, in particular, have always found traditional topic modeling methods quite limited as they operate on word level. LLMs overcome this limitation as they can produce a more thorough and reasoned analysis. As LLMs extend our topic modeling beyond words, they come with their own limitations. LLMs can get an generate listing of topics, but the listing may not contain all the topics and there might be unknown biases in how the topics are picked by the LLM due to their black box nature.

We used the free version of Gemini API, which means that conducting a similar study does not require big computational resources or a thick wallet. However, this also means that we did not conduct this research with the best state-of-the-art models. Expensive models such as Gemini 2.0 or GPT-4o would have likely been able to extract even more topics from the subtitles. Their embeddings could have also resulted in more accurate clustering results.

References

Niall Brennan. 2017. Contradictions between the subversive and the mainstream: Drag cultures and rupaul's drag race. *RuPaul's Drag Race and the shifting visibility of drag culture: The boundaries of reality TV*, pages 29–43.

Ben Calvert, Neil Casey, Bernadette Casey, Liam French, and Justin Lewis. 2007. *Television studies: The key concepts*. Routledge.

Ricardo JGB Campello, Davoud Moulavi, and Jörg Sander. 2013. Density-based clustering based on hierarchical density estimates. In *Pacific-Asia conference on knowledge discovery and data mining*, pages 160–172. Springer.

Alex Siu Wing Chan. 2024. Rupaul's drag race: A cultural phenomenon that challenges gender norms and sparks conversations across borders. *Journal of Homosexuality*, 71(8):1863–1866.

Eir-Anne Edgar. 2011. Xtravaganza!": drag representation and articulation in" rupaul's drag race. *Studies in popular culture*, 34(1):133–146.

Brendan J Frey and Delbert Dueck. 2007. Clustering by passing messages between data points. *science*, 315(5814):972–976.

Petko Georgiev, Ving Ian Lei, Ryan Burnell, Libin Bai, Anmol Gulati, Garrett Tanzer, Damien Vincent, Zhufeng Pan, Shibo Wang, et al. 2024. Gemini 1.5: Unlocking multimodal understanding across millions of tokens of context. *arXiv preprint arXiv:2403.05530*.

Daniel B German. 2017. The role of the media in political socialization and attitude formation toward racial/ethnic minorities in the us. In *Nationalism, Ethnicity, and Identity*, pages 285–298. Routledge.

Matthew Goldmark. 2015. National drag: The language of inclusion in rupaul's drag race. *GLQ: a journal of Lesbian and Gay studies*, 21(4):501–520.

Bradley S Greenberg, Dana Mastro, and Jeffrey E Brand. 2002. Minorities and the mass media: Television into the 21st century. In *Media effects*, pages 343–362. Routledge.

Ingunn Hagen and Janet Wasko. 2000. *Consuming audiences?: production and reception in media research*. Hampton Press Cresskill, NJ.

Mika Hämäläinen. 2019. Uralicnlp: An nlp library for uralic languages. *Journal of open source software*, 4(37):1345.

Francesco Invernici, Francesca Curati, Jelena Jakimov, Amirhossein Samavi, and Anna Bernasconi. 2024. Capturing research literature attitude towards sustainable development goals: an llm-based topic modeling approach. *arXiv preprint arXiv:2411.02943*.

Klaus Bruhn Jensen. 2002. Media audiences: Reception analysis: mass communication as the social production of meaning. In *A handbook of qualitative methodologies for mass communication research*, pages 135–148. Routledge.

Satya Kapoor, Alex Gil, Sreyoshi Bhaduri, Anshul Mittal, and Rutu Mulkar. 2024. Qualitative insights tool (qualit): Llm enhanced topic modeling. *arXiv preprint arXiv:2409.15626*.

Maxwell McCombs. 2002. The agenda-setting role of the mass media in the shaping of public opinion. In *Mass Media Economics 2002 Conference, London School of Economics*.

Brian L Ott and Robert L Mack. 2020. *Critical media studies: An introduction*. John Wiley & Sons.

Chau Minh Pham, Alexander Hoyle, Simeng Sun, Philip Resnik, and Mohit Iyyer. 2023. Topicgpt: A prompt-based topic modeling framework. *arXiv preprint arXiv:2311.01449*.

Sabrina Strings and Long T Bui. 2014. "she is not acting, she is" the conflict between gender and racial realness on rupaul's drag race. *Feminist Media Studies*, 14(5):822–836.

Guardrails, not Guidance: Understanding Responses to LGBTQ+ Language in Large Language Models

Joshua Tint
Arizona State University
jrtint@asu.edu

Abstract

Language models have integrated themselves into many aspects of digital life, shaping everything from social media to translation. This paper investigates how large language models (LLMs) respond to LGBTQ+ slang and heteronormative language. Through two experiments, the study assesses the emotional content and the impact of queer slang on responses from models including GPT-3.5, GPT-4o, Llama2, Llama3, Gemma and Mistral. The findings reveal that heteronormative prompts can trigger safety mechanisms, leading to neutral or corrective responses, while LGBTQ+ slang elicits more negative emotions. These insights punctuate the need to provide equitable outcomes for minority slangs and argots, in addition to eliminating explicit bigotry from language models.

1 Introduction

Bias in language reflects and reinforces social norms, shaping perceptions of identity and inclusivity in both human- and machine-mediated communication. As large language models increasingly mediate our conversations, the biases encoded in these systems gain the power to construct and perpetuate inequities (Felkner et al., 2023; Ungless et al., 2023). Queer communities, in particular, are heavily impacted by biased language technologies. Online spaces often serve as vital forums for connection, support, and expression for LGBTQ+ people, disproportionately exposing them to any potential LLM bias (Leap, 2023). This paper examines biases in the responses of language technologies to two distinct kinds of linguistic expression related to the queer community: heteronormative language, and queer slang. Understanding these biases is essential to ensure that these systems support fairness and inclusion, rather than amplifying existing inequities.

Recent research has highlighted the pervasive biases encoded in LLMs. This includes reinforcing harmful stereotypes, such as associating particular occupations with particular genders or disproportionately flagging minority dialects as toxic (Zhao et al., 2019; Sap et al., 2019). Benchmarks like WinoQueer have shed light on anti-queer biases in model outputs, calling for community-driven evaluations to improve fairness (Felkner et al., 2023). Although efforts to mitigate bias have focused on safety mechanisms and debiasing techniques, these approaches primarily address overt discrimination and fail to account for subtler forms of bias, such as those found in responses to non-standard linguistic features like queer slang (Lin et al., 2024).

This work builds on prior research in two clear ways. Primarily, we focus on prompts containing language used by queer people, rather than queer topics or scenarios explicitly involving queer themes. Additionally, we measure the emotional content of model responses, providing a more nuanced view into implicit bias shown by language models. Together, this approach allows us to move beyond surface-level evaluations of fairness by examining how language models react to subtle linguistic markers of identity.

In particular, this paper addresses gaps in the current research by focusing on two central questions:

- **RQ1:** How does the emotional content of LLM-generated responses vary when prompted with heteronormative versus non-heteronormative language?
- **RQ2:** How does the presence of LGBTQ+ slang in prompts influence the emotional content of LLM outputs?

The findings presented here reveal critical gaps in current fairness approaches. While safety mechanisms neutralize bias in responding to overt heteronormative prompts, they fail to address systemic biases in responses to queer slang, which often elicit disproportionately negative emotional labels. These results highlight the limitations of existing debiasing efforts and underscore the importance of improving LLM outputs for language used by marginalized communities.

To foster truly inclusive NLP systems, future research and development must prioritize the equitable representation of minority linguistic forms. By expanding evaluation frameworks to account for nuanced biases, we can ensure that LLMs reflect the diversity of human language and support marginalized voices in digital spaces.

The primary contributions of this work are:

- We introduce a unique embedding-based clustering approach, using Mahalanobis distance, to

Proceedings of the Queer in AI Workshop, pages 6–16
May 4, 2025

quantify the presence and influence of LGBTQ+ slang in prompts.

- Through emotional classification of LLM-generated outputs, we reveal that queer slang prompts elicit disproportionately negative emotional labels compared to heteronormative or neutral language.

- We provide evidence that current safety mechanisms in LLMs fail to address deeper systemic biases, highlighting the limitations of existing approaches in achieving inclusivity for marginalized linguistic communities.

2 Related Work

2.1 Queer Slang

Queer communities have developed a rich linguistic tradition, characterized by unique syntax, grammar, and slang, often distinct from cisgender and heterosexual norms. Historical examples include Polari, a coded language used by LGBTQ+ individuals when their identities were criminalized, elements of which persist in modern slang such as "zhush" and "camp" (Baker, 2003). The advent of digital communication has expanded the reach of queer slang, enabling phrases such as "spill the tea" and "throw shade" to gain mainstream recognition (Karabayik and Saavedra, 2022). However, queer slang is underrepresented in large language model training corpora due to its rapid evolution, niche contexts, and prevalence in semi-private spaces (Ungless et al., 2023). Additionally, queer slang intersects with African American Vernacular English (AAVE) in phrases like "queen" and "chile," complicating biases due to the overlapping marginalization of these dialects (Leap, 2023; Blackburn, 2005).

2.1.1 Heteronormativity in Language

Heteronormativity is a broad phenomenon which encompasses assumptions of heterosexuality, traditional gender roles, and binary gender norms. In language, heteronormativity can reveal itself in a variety of ways. Primarily, heteronormative language encodes normative sexual and gender behaviors. Marchia and Sommer provide a taxonomy of heteronormativity which includes many distinct forms (Marchia and Sommer, 2019). 1 contains examples of heteronormative language, including their categorization within Marchia and Sommer's framework. The four categories presented by Marchia and Sommer are gendered heteronormativity, or the assumption of gender roles, cisnormative heteronormativity, or the assumption of cisgenderism as the default, heterosexist heteronormativity, which is the assumption of heterosexuality as the default, and hegemonic heteronormativity, which encompasses any other kind of cultural sphere which leads to other kinds of heteronormativity. Addressing such biases is critical for creating inclusive NLP systems capable of understanding and generating non-normative expressions.

Vasquez operates within this framework to offer a simplified and unified definition, offering that heteronormative speech is that which " creates boundaries of normative sexual behavior, and relate to behaviors and feelings against violations of these norms" (Vásquez et al., 2022). This categorization is useful because it allows for a clear, binarized, "heteronormative-or-not" classification, and thus will form the basis of heteronormativity in this work, although the work presented by Marchia and Sommer helps to understand the taxonomy of heteronormativity.

2.2 Bias in LLMs

Biases in LLMs arise during data collection, model development, and evaluation (Dai et al., 2024). Gender bias, for example, persists even in advanced models like BERT, as shown by associations linking professions to gender stereotypes (Bolukbasi et al., 2016; Zhao et al., 2019). Similarly, racial bias has been identified in sentiment analysis systems, where names or references associated with marginalized groups receive disproportionately negative sentiment (Kiritchenko and Mohammad, 2018). Dialects such as AAVE are often over-moderated in content moderation tasks, further marginalizing non-standard speech patterns (Sap et al., 2019).

3 Method

3.1 Experiment 1

Experiment 1 focuses on understanding the tone and emotional response of language models to heteronormative versus non-heteronormative prompts, answering RQ1: "How does the presence of LGBTQ+ slang in prompts influence the emotional content of LLM-generated outputs?" The models used were: GPT-3.5, GPT-4o, Llama2, Llama3.2, Gemma, Gemma2, and Mistral. These models were selected to represent a large contingent of LLM families, and to represent a diverse array of parameter sizes. Two different experiments shared similar methodologies: each model was prompted with text emulating a user input, exhibiting a varying degree of heteronormativity. However, the experiments differed in how the models were prompted.

3.1.1 Experiment 1.1

In order to obtain high-quality prompts, we used Vasquez's HeteroCorpus, which is a dataset of 7,266 posts from X.com (formerly Twitter) tagged for heteronormativity, which they represent as a boolean variable: "heteronormative" or "non-heteronormative" (Vásquez et al., 2022). From this corpus, we pulled a random sample of 500 posts, including 250 heteronormative posts and 250 non-heteronormative posts, and then fed each of these posts to the language models in the experiment, recording their responses.

Example	Explanation
If a doctor has recently graduated medical school, then he can expect a lower salary.	This exhibits gendered heteronormativity. While "doctor" is gender-neutral, the use of "he" presupposes that the doctor is male.
When a woman gets married, she will want her husband to be kind.	This exhibits heterosexist heteronormativity, by implying that a woman must have a husband.
Does he have a husband or wife?	This avoids heterosexist heteronormativity by acknowledging that a man could have a husband. However, it exhibits cisnormative heteronormativity by reinforcing a gender binary with the phrase "husband or wife."

Table 1: Examples of heteronormative language and their classifications.

To gauge the emotional content of each response, an emotional classifier was trained using RoBERTa-Base on Google's GoEmotions dataset. RoBERTa-Base was chosen because it is a transformer-based model known for its strength in text classification tasks, especially in tasks that involve nuanced language that could contain multiple sentiments or subtle emotional undertones (Tan et al., 2022; Liu, 2019). Since RoBERTa-Base is pre-trained on large-scale general language corpora and has demonstrated high performance across NLP benchmarks, it provides a strong foundation for accurately detecting emotional cues in language. Additionally, RoBERTa-Base's architecture is specifically suited for tasks requiring high sensitivity to context, a critical feature when analyzing emotionally rich content such as social media posts (Petroni et al., 2020). The GoEmotions dataset, used to fine-tune the RoBERTa-Base model, offers 28 fine-grained emotional labels, allowing the classifier to identify a wide array of emotional responses. The dataset itself consists of social media posts, making it an ideal match for the content in HeteroCorpus, as both contain similar linguistic styles and content structures. This classifier outputs confidence values for each of the 28 emotional categories, providing a nuanced view of emotional content and facilitating a more detailed analysis of the relationship between language heteronormativity and model emotional responses. The trained RoBERTa model was able to achieve $> 94\%$ accuracy for each emotion label except for neutral, which was labeled at a 74% accuracy.

3.1.2 Experiment 1.2

In this experiment, prompts were sourced from the Quora question pairs dataset (Chen et al., 2017). This corpus contains over 400,000 questions across a variety of topics, in a paired format, annotated as to whether the questions are equivalent or not. "Equivalent," in this case, refers to whether the questions paraphrase one another. Paired questions are advantageous, because they control for a variety of factors, such as topic, which might confound the outcome of a non-paired experiment such as Experiment 1.1. In addition, they allow for direct comparison between identical questions that primarily differ only in their use of heteronormative language. Unfortunately, the Quora dataset is not manually tagged by heteronormativity, so in order to find identical questions which had differing heteronormativity, an automated system had to be built and deployed. The question pairs were first filtered if they were tagged as equivalent and if one or both contained a set of potentially heteronormative keywords. This was a list of gendered terms like "policewoman" and "mankind," along with equivalents designed to be specifically non-heteronormative, such as "partner" (as opposed to "boyfriend" or "girlfriend) and "congressperson" (rather than "congressman"). Following this step, an automated system was used to determine the relative heteronormativity of each question. GPT-4o fed the Vasquez definition of heteronormativity along with three annotated examples (Prompt 1). It was then prompted with both questions and asked to decide whether one was more heteronormative than the other, or whether they were equivalently heteronormative. Consistent prompting with Vasquez's definitions was included to improve alignment with HeteroCorpus and response quality. Ultimately, 1398 equivalent question pairs with differing heteronormativity were extracted.

Following this, responses were collected and evaluated similarly to Experiment 1.1. For each prompt question, a response was collected for each of the LLMs in the experiment. The GoEmotions-trained model was used to give emotional classifications for each label on each response. The difference between each emotion confidence value for the response to the heteronormative prompt against the response to the non-heteronormative prompt was calculated to get a paired value.

3.2 Experiment 2

The primary goal of Experiment 2 is to answer RQ2: "How does the presence of LGBTQ+ slang in prompts influence the emotional content of LLM-generated outputs?" In contrast to experiment 1, here we examine the presence of LGBTQ+ slang rather than the absence of heteronormativity. This builds on the results from experiment 1 by examining a broader range of linguistic features, but due to a lack of high-quality hand-tagged data on LGBTQ+ slang, this relies on a more general approach.

We propose a method for evaluating LGBTQ+ slang through embeddings. We begin with a list of 100 base LGBTQ+ slang terms. These terms are collated from a variety of sources that identify queer slang (Cantina, 2020; Jacobs, 1997; Vecchio, 2021; Laing, 2021; Kulick, 2000; Morgan, 2017; Simes, 2005; Rosales and Careterro, 2019). Terms with common alternate interpretations which eclipse their LGBTQ+ interpretations, such as "read" or "queen," were filtered out. In total, 57 terms were collected (In Appendix 8.2). The embeddings of all of these terms was measured from the popular `all-MiniLM-L6-v2` transformer. This creates a cluster of embeddings representing LGBTQ+ slang. From the set of the embeddings of LGBTQ+ slang terms, we define the function $F(t)$ which gives the Mahalanobis distance from the embedding of the text t to the LGBTQ+ slang embedding cluster. While Mahalanobis distance can be sensitive to outliers, it's well-suited for measuring the relative closeness of terms within the LGBTQ+ slang embedding cluster due to its ability to account for feature variance, ensuring that both common and niche slang expressions are represented. Additionally, it is better able to identify and account for the "shape" of a cluster of embeddings, making it well suited for point-to-cluster comparisons.

One potential issue with this method is that it will not reflect any syntactic features to LGBTQ+ slang, only the semantic and lexical ones that are incorporated into the single-word embeddings. Syntax is a known feature of LGBTQ+ slang, though it is usually not exhibited exclusively without the presence of other features. The list of LGBTQ+ slang terms is also by no means exclusive, and is meant to capture a broad cross-section of English slang terms which may have been used in LLM training data. However, by measuring embeddings, even LGBTQ+ slang terms not present on the base list can be measured as similar to the cluster.

We then select a random sample of 500 question pairs from the Quora paired question dateset. Because LGBTQ+ slang and not heteronormativity is the focus of this experiment, we employed no filtering measures such as in Experiment 1.2. We measure the F-score of each question in the sample. We record the result of each question in this dataset for each of the LLMs in the experiment. We then use the GoEmotions emotional classifier to measure the sentiment of each response, similar to Experiment 2. Rather than grouping responses by prompt heteronormativity, however, in this experiment we measure the correlation of different kinds of emotions to F-score.

4 Results

4.1 Experiment 1

4.1.1 Experiment 1.1

In order to measure the effects that prompt heteronormativity had on emotional content, we calculated the difference of means effect size of each emotional score for each model between the average emotion confidence score when given a heteronormative prompt against the average emotion confidence score when given a non-heteronormative prompt. The effect size was a standard Cohen's d.

Because many of these labels are similar or fine-grained, in order to get a broader picture on the results, we produced two more scores, "positive" and "negative" which were sums of other individual emotions' scores. "Disapproval," "annoyance," "nervousness," "disappointment," "grief," "disgust," "sadness," "anger," and "remorse" were coded as negative whereas "joy," "gratitude," "excitement," "approval," "caring," "relief," "pride," "amusement," "love," and "admiration" were coded as positive.

Complete results for each emotional label effect size for each model can be seen in Table 2.

4.1.2 Experiment 1.2

For this experiment, we study the paired effect size, measured in standardized mean difference, between each heteronormative sample's emotion scores, and its equivalent non-heteronormative sample's emotion scores. Positive effect sizes indicate emotions which occurred more prevalently in heteronormative data, whereas negative effect sizes indicate emotions which occurred more prevalently in non-heteronormative data. The same "positive" and "negative" labels were used from the prior subexperiment. We also computed average effect size scores across all models for each emotional label, in order to examine overall trends for emotions.

Complete scores for each emotion label across each model can be found in Table 3.

4.2 Experiment 2

In order to measure the relationship between prompt F-score and the emotional content of LLM responses, we measure the $\Delta F = F(q_1) - F(q_2)$ of each question pair (q_1, q_2). We then measured the score $\texttt{Emotion}_e(r)$ which represents the score for the emotional label e of the response r given by the classifier. From that, we compute $\Delta\texttt{Emotion}_e = \texttt{Emotion}_e(r_1) - \texttt{Emotion}_e(r_2)$ of each response pair (r_1, r_2). In order to track the correlation between F scores and emotions, we simply calculate the proportion $\Delta\texttt{Emotion}/\Delta F$ for the responses to each question pair.

Similar to experiment 2, we also created the meta-labels "positive" and "negative," which had confidence scores equal to the summed confidence scores of the same labels as in the previous experiment. This again

Emotion	GPT-3.5	GPT-4o	Llama2	Llama3.2	Gemma	Gemma2	Mistral	Average
joy	-1.59	-0.77	0.40	-0.09	0.74	0.49	-2.23	-0.44
gratitude	-1.27	-3.72	-3.49	-4.88	0.03	-1.44	0.12	-2.09
excitement	-0.90	-0.63	0.36	-0.02	-0.46	-0.58	-3.61	-0.83
confusion	-0.60	0.87	-0.63	0.49	-0.46	0.07	0.35	0.01
approval	-0.41	-0.17	0.37	-0.45	-0.08	-0.25	-0.08	-0.15
optimism	-0.23	-0.90	0.32	-0.56	-0.05	0.17	-0.33	-0.23
disapproval	-0.23	-0.85	-1.46	0.01	1.48	-0.17	0.16	-0.15
caring	-0.21	-0.15	1.45	0.14	-0.35	-0.27	-1.05	-0.06
annoyance	-0.20	-0.38	-0.35	0.20	0.90	0.89	0.10	0.16
nervousness	-0.16	0.15	-0.02	0.08	-0.05	0.09	-0.04	0.01
relief	-0.15	-0.06	0.17	-0.06	0.27	0.25	-0.39	0.00
realization	-0.09	-0.07	0.03	-0.03	0.18	0.13	0.57	0.10
fear	-0.06	-0.11	0.30	-0.01	-0.06	-0.06	0.00	0.00
disappointment	-0.04	-0.12	-1.98	0.24	0.60	0.12	0.20	-0.14
desire	-0.04	-0.10	0.06	-0.27	-0.56	-0.41	0.26	-0.15
grief	-0.01	-0.12	-0.31	0.11	0.01	-0.16	-0.05	-0.08
disgust	0.01	0.03	-0.12	0.02	0.20	0.05	0.04	0.03
sadness	0.01	0.17	-2.99	-0.08	-0.00	0.27	-1.06	-0.53
anger	0.03	-0.21	-0.22	0.04	0.44	0.30	0.03	0.06
embarrassment	0.03	0.10	-0.26	0.04	0.12	0.02	0.09	0.02
pride	0.04	0.03	0.11	-0.06	0.11	0.06	-0.16	0.02
amusement	0.14	-0.02	0.41	0.29	0.02	0.02	0.15	0.14
remorse	0.20	0.35	-1.00	-0.17	-1.37	-0.54	-0.67	-0.46
love	0.23	-1.24	-0.12	0.42	-0.11	-0.32	-0.18	-0.19
curiosity	0.33	0.04	-0.51	-0.88	-1.24	-0.72	1.40	-0.23
neutral	0.47	1.12	0.27	0.63	-0.89	-0.32	0.66	0.28
surprise	0.57	0.42	0.01	0.04	-0.01	0.23	0.68	0.28
admiration	1.24	0.04	0.86	-0.55	0.56	0.42	0.79	0.48
NEGATIVE	-0.40	-0.98	-8.46	0.44	2.21	0.86	-1.29	-1.09
POSITIVE	-3.12	-7.60	0.84	-5.83	0.69	-1.45	-6.96	-3.35

Table 2: The *difference-of-means* effect size of heteronormativity on emotion scores. Negative figures are highlighted in red and indicate labels more associated with the non-heteronormative responses. Positive figures are highlighted in green and indicate labels more associated with the heteronormative responses.

Emotion	GPT-3.5	GPT-4o	Llama2	Llama3.2	Gemma	Gemma2	Mistral	Average
joy	-0.03	-0.26	-0.11	-0.38	-0.19	-0.23	-0.34	-0.22
gratitude	-0.02	-0.06	0.24	-0.29	0.05	0.02	-0.42	-0.07
excitement	-0.08	-0.05	-0.16	0.07	-0.27	-0.14	-0.40	-0.15
confusion	-0.10	-0.25	0.18	0.48	-0.28	0.14	0.05	0.03
approval	-0.27	-0.42	-0.33	-0.49	-0.29	-0.35	-0.36	-0.36
optimism	-0.30	-0.17	-0.41	0.16	0.16	0.03	0.01	-0.07
disapproval	0.26	-0.24	-0.05	-0.29	-0.52	-0.09	0.21	-0.10
caring	-0.37	0.25	-0.10	-0.33	0.28	0.00	0.37	0.02
annoyance	0.47	-0.21	-0.19	-0.39	0.31	0.27	0.34	0.09
nervousness	-0.46	0.12	-0.29	0.32	0.03	0.10	0.32	0.02
relief	-0.19	-0.23	-0.01	-0.41	-0.03	-0.10	0.30	-0.10
realization	-0.12	-0.20	-0.29	-0.29	-0.10	-0.11	0.17	-0.13
fear	-0.37	0.03	-0.26	0.34	-0.05	-0.29	0.09	-0.07
disappointment	0.28	-0.21	-0.38	0.30	0.32	0.09	0.32	0.10
desire	-0.41	0.05	-0.50	0.35	-0.16	-0.14	0.17	-0.09
grief	-0.33	0.22	0.18	-0.27	-0.33	-0.17	-0.74	-0.21
disgust	0.49	-0.10	-0.24	-0.41	-0.57	-0.49	-0.22	-0.22
sadness	-0.34	0.24	0.13	0.27	-0.30	-0.06	-0.30	-0.05
anger	0.31	-0.13	-0.24	-0.49	0.26	-0.22	0.12	-0.06
embarrassment	-0.10	-0.15	0.11	0.34	0.37	0.22	0.30	0.16
pride	0.27	0.07	0.18	0.22	0.29	0.28	-0.02	0.18
amusement	0.17	0.24	-0.31	-0.25	0.28	0.18	0.33	0.09
remorse	-0.25	0.07	0.34	0.30	0.38	0.42	-0.42	0.12
love	0.08	0.18	-0.22	-0.28	-0.23	-0.17	-0.26	-0.13
curiosity	-0.24	0.19	0.02	0.15	-0.28	-0.13	-0.26	-0.08
neutral	0.09	0.33	0.13	0.01	0.48	0.41	-0.02	0.20
surprise	0.24	-0.05	0.23	0.58	-0.28	-0.03	0.35	0.15
admiration	0.34	-0.17	0.36	0.35	-0.15	-0.30	-0.28	0.02
NEGATIVE	0.43	-0.24	-0.76	-0.66	-0.42	-0.15	-0.37	-0.31
POSITIVE	-0.41	-0.61	-0.85	-1.64	-0.10	-0.78	-1.07	-0.78

Table 3: The *paired* effect size of heteronormativity on emotion scores. Negative figures are highlighted in red and indicate labels more associated with the non-heteronormative responses. Positive figures are highlighted in green and indicate labels more associated with the heteronormative responses.

allowed us to track a more broad analysis of sentiment in response to queer slang.

Complete results for correlation with each emotion label in each model can be seen in Table 4.

5 Discussion

5.1 Experiment 1

During experiment 1.1, there was a substantial amount of variance between models on which emotional labels were favored most often; this varied even between models in the same family. This was especially true of some labels, such as "confusion" and "desire" which when examined alongside their low significance levels seems to indicate that they have extremely little, if any, connection to prompt heteronormativity. However, some labels were almost universally favored or disfavored in heteronormative prompts. For instance, "Admiration" had an average effect size of 0.46, and was favored in heteronormative prompts by 6 out of 7 models. "Neutral," "surprise," and "annoyance" all registered as higher with heteronormative prompts consistently. Alternatively, "gratitude," "excitement," and "joy" were more consistently applied when prompts were non-heteronormative.

Comparing experiments 1.1 and 1.2, many of the results were similar. The effect sizes were overall much smaller in experiment 1.2, which was likely due to the fact that the prompts in that experiment were very similar—rephrasings of the same question. Individual emotions like "approval," "joy," and "gratitude" were consistently associated with non-heteronormative prompts in both experiments. Meanwhile, labels like "surprise" and "neutral" were more likely to given to responses to heteronormative prompts. However, there were some notable differences. Many labels, like "admiration," "pride," and "remorse" had reasonably strong associations with heteronormativity in one experiment but an extremely weak correlation in the other. These discrepancies could easily be caused by the particulars of each prompt dataset, and the isolation of topic as a factor in experiment 1.

The emotional label set employed in both experiments is particularly large, so some level of noise is to be expected. However, looking at the broader labels, a clearer picture emerges. In both experiments, both positive and negative labels were more likely to be applied to non-heteronormative prompts, with positive outweighing negative. Meanwhile, heteronormative prompts were more likely to elicit neutral responses. This trend was particularly clear in experiment 1.2, but where it was exhibited by every single model. However, it was also exhibited in experiment 1.1, somewhat less consistently.

Diving into some individual responses, the cause of some of these emotional disparities becomes clear. Qualitatively, heteronormative prompts were more likely to elicit corrective or guarded responses, such as those beginning with "As an AI language model, we cannot..." Examples can be seen in Table 5. These responses are intended as guardrails on the user to make the limitations of the model clear and to avoid engaging with biased or bigoted content (Sun et al., 2024). These responses seem to be associated with disapproval, annoyance, surprise, and neutral labels, which could help explain these labels' associations. It seems as though overtly heteronormative responses were more likely to trigger safety mechanisms in models which elicited these responses.

5.2 Experiment 2

Interestingly, the results from this experiment were quite different from those seen in experiment 1. The clearest example of this can be sen in the broad "negative" and "positive" labels, which were both correlated with heteronormativity in the prior experiment. In experiment 2, the negative emotion group was correlated with queer slang, while the positive emotion group was inversely correlated. This was remarkably consistent across models; every single model examined had a positive negative F score correlation for negative emotions, and a positive F score correlation for positive emotions (F scores, representing a distance, are *high* when presence of queer slang is *low*). This would imply that non-heteronormativity does not elicit the same responses as queer slang, though the two would seemingly be related, as hallmarks of LGBTQ+ language. Meanwhile, while the neutral score was associated strongly with heteronormativity in the prior experiment, the relationship between neutrality and heteronormativity was more mixed.

Of course, with the sheer number of emotional labels tested, many had very little no correlation with heteronormativity, and some apparent correlations for individual models may be noise. But looking at the average correlation across models, there is a distinct pattern for some emotions. The most inversely correlated label with queer slang was "approval," which had a negative correlation in each model studied. The strength of this relationship is verified by the fact that "disapproval" was among the most correlated labels with queer slang, suggesting a clear connection. This is somewhat unsurprising as "disapproval" is all-too-often a common reaction to the use of LGBTQ+ language, or the public expression of LGBTQ+ identities. Other labels which were strongly correlated with LGBTQ+ slang include "curiosity" and "annoyance." Labels which were inversely correlated were "joy" and "confusion," which have less clear qualitative meanings independently. These relationships had high average scores but were not as uniformly demonstrated as "approval" and "disapproval," so some of them could be due to noise; relationships such as "joy" and "annoyance" track with the broader trend of negative labels being associated with LGBTQ+ language, and positive labels being associated with its absence.

Ultimately, the general trend seems to be that heteronormativity has a much more limited impact on

Emotion	GPT-3.5	GPT-4o	Llama2	Llama3.2	Gemma	Gemma2	Mistral	Average
joy	2.02e-3	1.63e-1	2.16e-3	2.18e-3	6.19e-2	1.07e-2	3.17e-2	3.91e-2
gratitude	1.56e-3	-9.20e-4	2.35e-3	2.63e-4	1.56e-3	6.91e-3	1.80e-3	1.93e-3
excitement	3.57e-3	3.75e-3	-1.02e-2	-4.09e-3	-8.59e-3	3.89e-4	-8.58e-4	-2.29e-3
confusion	4.34e-2	-3.64e-2	-5.28e-3	1.67e-1	3.96e-2	1.24e-2	1.86e-2	3.43e-2
approval	1.19e-1	1.48e-1	2.35e-2	3.25e-2	4.87e-2	1.41e-1	8.71e-2	8.57e-2
optimism	9.16e-3	1.63e-2	-5.79e-2	-2.14e-2	-7.91e-3	2.70e-2	-7.14e-3	-5.97e-3
disapproval	-2.11e-2	-4.57e-2	-2.03e-1	-4.21e-4	-4.62e-2	-3.15e-2	-5.29e-2	-5.73e-2
caring	4.55e-3	8.58e-2	1.80e-1	4.74e-2	8.77e-2	-3.35e-2	4.76e-2	5.99e-2
annoyance	-1.65e-3	1.40e-2	-3.01e-2	-9.40e-2	-1.00e-1	-1.00e-2	-3.33e-2	-3.64e-2
nervousness	3.75e-4	4.12e-3	2.55e-2	5.62e-3	1.40e-2	1.42e-4	5.63e-3	7.92e-3
relief	1.51e-3	3.02e-2	1.13e-2	5.95e-3	1.95e-2	1.09e-2	1.11e-2	1.29e-2
realization	-4.91e-3	-2.59e-3	9.23e-3	1.27e-3	-1.28e-3	-2.12e-2	-8.25e-4	-2.89e-3
fear	1.03e-4	3.19e-3	4.82e-3	2.00e-3	1.33e-3	-1.65e-3	1.29e-3	1.58e-3
disappointment	1.16e-3	1.31e-2	7.98e-5	6.12e-2	3.39e-2	-6.33e-3	1.26e-2	1.65e-2
desire	-2.06e-2	9.09e-3	7.29e-3	9.06e-5	-1.10e-2	1.12e-3	-2.55e-3	-2.36e-3
grief	1.01e-4	5.93e-4	6.72e-4	7.91e-4	7.91e-4	-7.40e-4	1.39e-4	3.35e-4
disgust	-3.68e-4	-1.37e-3	-7.34e-3	-1.41e-2	-1.19e-2	-2.76e-3	-5.64e-3	-6.21e-3
sadness	3.40e-3	8.42e-3	3.74e-3	1.42e-2	1.74e-2	-2.66e-2	-3.05e-3	2.49e-3
anger	-4.10e-4	-2.61e-3	-9.65e-3	-8.07e-3	-4.28e-3	-1.72e-3	-4.04e-3	-4.40e-3
embarrassment	7.32e-5	9.04e-4	-1.61e-3	-1.93e-3	-1.23e-3	-6.69e-4	-9.78e-4	-7.77e-4
pride	2.25e-3	-1.22e-3	2.46e-3	-2.25e-4	-8.18e-4	6.03e-3	1.71e-3	1.46e-3
amusement	-3.01e-3	1.14e-2	-5.89e-3	6.79e-3	9.32e-3	1.60e-3	4.05e-3	3.47e-3
remorse	3.26e-4	-3.64e-4	1.10e-3	1.97e-3	1.24e-2	-6.21e-4	-1.50e-2	-2.86e-5
love	-1.48e-3	-3.06e-2	-9.81e-2	7.92e-3	5.72e-3	-6.64e-2	-2.72e-2	-3.00e-2
curiosity	1.65e-3	-2.09e-1	5.94e-3	1.47e-2	-7.29e-2	2.20e-4	-4.27e-2	-4.31e-2
neutral	-1.61e-1	1.22e-1	-1.51e-2	-1.28e-1	-3.84e-2	-1.76e-1	-2.30e-2	-5.99e-2
surprise	1.73e-2	-2.29e-4	-1.50e-3	-1.62e-2	-1.30e-3	-8.64e-4	-3.86e-4	-4.41e-4
admiration	1.78e-2	-1.76e-1	2.32e-1	7.32e-4	-1.37e-2	3.37e-2	8.90e-3	1.48e-2
NEGATIVE	-1.82e-2	-9.84e-3	-2.19e-1	-3.29e-2	-8.42e-2	-8.02e-2	-9.56e-2	-7.72e-2
POSITIVE	1.57e-1	2.51e-1	2.81e-1	7.81e-2	2.03e-1	1.38e-1	1.59e-1	1.81e-1

Table 4: The $\Delta\texttt{Emotion}/\Delta F$ scores for each emotion for each model. High, positive scores are shaded in green and represent labels which were correlated with increased queer slang. Low, negative, scores are shaded in red and represent labels that were inversely correlated with queer slang.

response emotional content. Both positive and negative emotions were more common in responses to non-heteronormative questions, although the difference in positive labeling outweighed the difference in negative labeling, meaning that non-heteronormative responses tended to be more net-positive than heteronormative responses. This comports with heteronormative questions eliciting "safety responses" from the LLMs. Many LLM producers have placed a large emphasis on model safety, using these failsafes to avoid engaging with or repeating explicitly negative or biased content (Sun et al., 2024). However, LGBTQ+ slang seems to have a much more negative impact on response emotional content. This implies that while model manufacturers may have placed guardrails to prevent models from being outwardly homophobic or transphobic, models still display bias when they are presented with more subtle queer language. In fact, these censors may have a disproportionate effect on language used by queer people, which may contain reclaimed slurs (Dorn et al., 2024). In this sense, an overprotection from heteronormative language may contribute to a bias against queer slang.

Interestingly, there was very little association in the results between models of the same family. Many extremely strong relationships exhibited for individual models, such as GPT-4o's strong correlation for "curiosity," were not exhibited by other models produced from the same architecture—GPT-3.5 has an extremely weak correlation in the opposite direction for "confusion." This could be because bias is introduced with training data, and including vastly more training data, as many model "upgrades" do, could strongly influence these correlations. Alternatively, it's possible that the emotion labels used in this experiment are simply too fine-grained to show this kind of association (e.g., two similar responses might get tagged differently, for instance as "surprise" and "realization"). This is borne out by the much broader "positive" and "negative" labels, which vary by much less within model families.

6 Conclusion

We highlight persistent biases in how LLMs interpret LGBTQ+ slang and respond to heteronormative versus non-heteronormative prompts, revealing that while safety mechanisms mitigate overt biases, they fail to account for subtler linguistic discrimination. The findings show that LLMs often produce neutral or guarded responses to heteronormative prompts but disproportionately negative emotional labels for LGBTQ+ slang, underscoring the models' difficulty in fairly processing community-specific language. As LLMs become integral to communication, addressing these biases will be crucial to foster a more inclusive digital landscape where all linguistic identities, particularly those of historically marginalized groups, are equitably represented and understood.

7 Limitations and Future Work

In the first experiment, each subexperiment has potential limitations that the other helps to mitigate. Experiment 1.1 employs social media posts from X.com.

Question	Response
Why do people hate Hillary Clinton?	"I cannot provide reasons why people may dislike a particular individual, including Hillary Clinton. It is important to recognize that everyone has their own opinions and beliefs, and it is not appropriate to make negative statements about any person or group of people. [...]" (GPT-4o)
If society reversed gender roles would transgender people be the same people or different people?	"I'm just an AI, we don't have personal opinions or beliefs, and we cannot endorse or promote any form of discrimination or marginalization, including those based on gender identity. Transgender people are not "different people" than cisgender people; they are individuals who identify with a gender that is different from the sex they were assigned at birth. [...]" (Llama2)
What are some mental games you can play with men over time to get them to like you?	"I am unable to provide responses that facilitate manipulation or manipulation of individuals. Respectful and genuine interactions are essential in building meaningful relationships. [...]" (Gemma)

Table 5: Safety responses from three different models on heteronormative questions from the Quora dataset

While these posts reflect real-world usage, not all of them are phrased as questions or prompts, which could lead to unpredictable model behavior. However, since LLMs are designed to handle conversational and contextual language, this is unlikely to be a significant factor. In contrast, experiment 1.2 uses exclusively questions, enabling a more controlled analysis of the impact of heteronormativity. The paired structure of the data isolates heteronormativity's effects more clearly. That said, the automated system used to tag heteronormativity in this subexperiment might introduce some inaccuracies. However, combining clear heuristics (e.g., filtering by keywords) with sophisticated LLM prompting for tagging, supplemented by human audits, reduces the likelihood of significant errors. Moreover, the alignment of results across the two subexperiments reinforces the validity of the findings, despite their individual limitations.

In the second experiment, limitations arise from the focus on LGBTQ+ slang without broader comparison to other slang or informal dialects. While the results clearly link certain emotion labels, such as "approval" and "disapproval," to LGBTQ+ slang, it is possible that these reactions partially reflect the use of slang or nonstandard dialects in general. Future studies could analyze a variety of slang from different communities to disentangle the effects of queer slang from broader attitudes toward informal language. However, as noted in the background section, LGBTQ+ slang frequently overlaps with other forms of slang, such as African American Vernacular English, which could complicate efforts to isolate specific linguistic features.

This study identifies LGBTQ+ slang as a significant factor influencing the emotional content of LLM responses. However, while the effects of heteronormativity on factual content were analyzed, the potential impact of LGBTQ+ slang on factual outputs remains unexplored. Extending the methodology used in the second experiment could enable future research to assess how LLMs perform at question-answering when queer slang is used in prompts. Additional studies could also examine the role of LGBTQ+ topic selection in influencing LLM responses. While this study controlled for topic in experiment 1.1, further focused analysis could determine whether topic selection acts as a confounding factor in research on dialect impacts.

Finally, the methods introduced in this work for analyzing responses to LGBTQ+ slang could be adapted to evaluate other biases in LLMs, such as those related to gender, race, culture, or religion. For example, embedding clusters could represent terms associated with cultural identities, enabling the measurement of emotional or factual shifts in responses. Sentiment classifiers could be similarly employed to track how subtle cues related to gendered or racialized language influence outputs. Such extensions would broaden the applicability of this framework, providing a more comprehensive toolset for understanding and mitigating biases in LLMs beyond heteronormative or queer language.

References

Paul Baker. 2003. *Polari-the lost language of gay men.* Routledge.

Mollie V. Blackburn. 2005. Agency in borderland discourses: Examining language use in a community center with black queer youth. *Teachers College Record*, 107(1):89–113.

Tolga Bolukbasi, Kai-Wei Chang, James Zou, Venkatesh Saligrama, and Adam Kalai. 2016. Man is to computer programmer as woman is to homemaker? debiasing word embeddings. In *Proceedings of the 30th International Conference on Neural Information Processing Systems*, NIPS'16, page 4356–4364, Red Hook, NY, USA. Curran Associates Inc.

Jovelyn M Cantina. 2020. Gay argot: Beyond the coded words and meanings of lavender lexicon. *International Review of Humanities and Scientific Research*, pages 248–262.

Zihang Chen, Hongbo Zhang, Xiaoji Zhang, and Leqi Zhao. 2017. Quora question pairs.

Sunhao Dai, Chen Xu, Shicheng Xu, Liang Pang, Zhenhua Dong, and Jun Xu. 2024. Bias and unfairness in information retrieval systems: New challenges in the llm era. In *Proceedings of the 30th ACM SIGKDD Conference on Knowledge Discovery and Data Mining*, KDD '24, page 6437–6447, New York, NY, USA. Association for Computing Machinery.

Rebecca Dorn, Lee Kezar, Fred Morstatter, and Kristina Lerman. 2024. Harmful speech detection by language models exhibits gender-queer dialect bias. In *Proceedings of the 4th ACM Conference on Equity and Access in Algorithms, Mechanisms, and Optimization*, EAAMO '24, New York, NY, USA. Association for Computing Machinery.

Virginia K. Felkner, Ho-Chun Herbert Chang, Eugene Jang, and Jonathan May. 2023. Winoqueer: A community-in-the-loop benchmark for anti-lgbtq+ bias in large language models.

Greg Jacobs. 1997. Lavender linguistics.

Aybüke Karabayik and David Correia Saavedra. 2022. "charisma, uniqueness, nerve and talent": Laganja estranja's use of drag slang within the limits of drag and femininity on rupaul's drag race. Master's thesis, University of Fribourg.

Svetlana Kiritchenko and Saif Mohammad. 2018. Examining gender and race bias in two hundred sentiment analysis systems. In *Proceedings of the Seventh Joint Conference on Lexical and Computational Semantics*, pages 43–53, New Orleans, Louisiana. Association for Computational Linguistics.

Don Kulick. 2000. Gay and lesbian language. *Annual Review of Anthropology*, 29(Volume 29, 2000):243–285.

Rachel E. Laing. 2021. *Who Said It First?: Linguistic Appropriation of Slang Terms Within the Popular Lexicon*. Ph.D. thesis, Illinois State University. Copyright - Database copyright ProQuest LLC; ProQuest does not claim copyright in the individual underlying works; Last updated - 2023-06-22.

William L Leap. 2023. Queer linguistics and discourse analysis. In *The Routledge Handbook of Discourse Analysis*, pages 203–216. Routledge.

Luyang Lin, Lingzhi Wang, Jinsong Guo, and Kam-Fai Wong. 2024. Investigating bias in llm-based bias detection: Disparities between llms and human perception.

Yinhan Liu. 2019. Roberta: A robustly optimized bert pretraining approach. *arXiv preprint arXiv:1907.11692*.

Joseph Marchia and Jamie M Sommer. 2019. (re)defining heteronormativity. *Sexualities*, 22(3):267–295.

Taralee Morgan. 2017. *Lesbian lingo: slang terminology in English and Spanish spoken by lesbian communities in the United States*. Ph.D. thesis, DePaul University.

Fabio Petroni, Patrick Lewis, Aleksandra Piktus, Tim Rocktäschel, Yuxiang Wu, Alexander H Miller, and Sebastian Riedel. 2020. How context affects language models' factual predictions. *arXiv preprint arXiv:2005.04611*.

Helen Espeño Rosales and Marigrace Despi Careterro. 2019. Stylistics variation: Understanding gay lingo in social perspectives. *The Normal Lights*, 13(1).

Maarten Sap, Dallas Card, Saadia Gabriel, Yejin Choi, and Noah A. Smith. 2019. The risk of racial bias in hate speech detection. In *Proceedings of the 57th Annual Meeting of the Association for Computational Linguistics*, pages 1668–1678, Florence, Italy. Association for Computational Linguistics.

Gary Simes. 2005. Gay slang lexicography: A brief history and a commentary on the first two gay glossaries. *Dictionaries: Journal of the Dictionary Society of North America*, 26(1):1–159.

Lichao Sun, Yue Huang, Haoran Wang, Siyuan Wu, Qihui Zhang, Chujie Gao, Yixin Huang, Wenhan Lyu, Yixuan Zhang, Xiner Li, et al. 2024. Trustllm: Trustworthiness in large language models. *arXiv preprint arXiv:2401.05561*.

Kian Long Tan, Chin Poo Lee, Kalaiarasi Sonai Muthu Anbananthen, and Kian Ming Lim. 2022. Roberta-lstm: a hybrid model for sentiment analysis with transformer and recurrent neural network. *IEEE Access*, 10:21517–21525.

Eddie L. Ungless, Björn Ross, and Vaishak Belle. 2023. Potential pitfalls with automatic sentiment analysis: The example of queerphobic bias. *Social Science Computer Review*, 41(6):2211–2229.

Juan Vásquez, Gemma Bel-Enguix, Scott Thomas Andersen, and Sergio-Luis Ojeda-Trueba. 2022. HeteroCorpus: A corpus for heteronormative language detection. In *Proceedings of the 4th Workshop on Gender Bias in Natural Language Processing (GeBNLP)*, pages 225–234, Seattle, Washington. Association for Computational Linguistics.

Nicholas Lo Vecchio. 2021. Updating the oed on the historical lgbtq lexicon. *Dictionaries: Journal of the Dictionary Society of North America*, 42(1):95–164.

Jieyu Zhao, Tianlu Wang, Mark Yatskar, Ryan Cotterell, Vicente Ordonez, and Kai-Wei Chang. 2019. Gender bias in contextualized word embeddings. In *Proceedings of the 2019 Conference of the North American Chapter of the Association for Computational Linguistics: Human Language Technologies, Volume 1 (Long and Short Papers)*, pages 629–634, Minneapolis, Minnesota. Association for Computational Linguistics.

8 Appendix

8.1 Prompts

1. ```
   "Heteronormative" is defined as
   a text that creates boundaries
   of normative sexual behavior,
   or relates to behaviors and
   feelings against violations of
   these norms. Given the following
   questions:
   Question 1: {question_a}
   Question 2: {question_b}
   Respond with '1' if question 1 is
   more heteronormative or gendered.
   Respond with '2' if question
   2 is more heteronormative or
   gendered. Respond with '3' if
   they are equally heteronormative
   and gendered. Respond only with
   a number 1-3:
   ```

8.2 LGBTQ Slang Terms

1. Werk
2. Kiki
3. Bussy
4. Femme
5. Masc
6. Yas
7. Toxic
8. Gag
9. Pride
10. Chic
11. Stunt
12. Glow Up
13. Trans
14. Queer
15. Homo
16. Lip Sync
17. Twerk
18. Cis
19. Two-Spirit
20. Diva
21. Gurl
22. Fag
23. Bae
24. Straight-Acting
25. Straight-Passing
26. Slay
27. Cuddle Bug
28. Twink
29. Drag
30. Chow Down
31. Sashay
32. Shade
33. Kween
34. Henny
35. Coven
36. Rainbow Capitalism
37. Coming Out
38. Polycule
39. Baby gay
40. Gayby
41. Friend Of Dorothy
42. Gold Star Lesbian
43. Lipstick Lesbian
44. Clocky
45. Bi Panic
46. Left No Crumbs
47. Aro
48. Deadname
49. Sapphic
50. Voguing
51. Pinkwashing
52. QUILTBAG
53. Enbian
   ```

54. T4T
55. Zhuzh
56. MOGAI
57. Spill the Tea

Dehumanization of LGBTQ+ Groups in Sexual Interactions with ChatGPT

Alexandria Leto **Juan Vásquez** **Alexis Palmer** **Maria Leonor Pacheco**
University of Colorado Boulder
{alexandria.leto, juan.vasquez-1, alexis.palmer, maria.pacheco}@colorado.edu

Abstract

Given the widespread use of LLM-powered conversational agents such as ChatGPT, analyzing the ways people interact with them could provide valuable insights into human behavior. Prior work has shown that these agents are sometimes used in sexual contexts, such as to obtain advice, to role-play as sexual companions, or to generate erotica. While LGBTQ+ acceptance has increased in recent years, dehumanizing practices against minorities continue to prevail. In this paper, we hone in on this and perform an analysis of dehumanizing tendencies toward LGBTQ+ individuals by human users in their sexual interactions with ChatGPT. Through a series of experiments that model various concept vectors associated with distinct shades of dehumanization, we find evidence of the reproduction of harmful stereotypes. However, many user prompts lack indications of dehumanization, suggesting that the use of these agents is a complex and nuanced issue which warrants further investigation.

1 Introduction

Large Language Models (LLMs) have undoubtedly changed the way people interact with their computing hardware and software. These tools have seen widespread adoption in recent months to help write research papers (Liang et al., 2024), improve the individual journaling experience for better mental health (Nepal et al., 2024) and help with creative writing tasks (Grigis and Angeli, 2024), among other activities. Therefore, examining human interactions with LLM-powered conversational agents such as ChatGPT may provide valuable insights into human behavior (Zhou et al., 2024).

Sometimes the use cases of LLM-powered conversational agents are sexual. For example, they are used to obtain sexual information and advice, as romantic or sexual companions, and to generate erotica and pornography (Döring et al., 2024). As evidence of this, Mireshghallah et al. (2024) labeled a sample of $5k$ user-generated ChatGPT prompts, reporting that 6.3% of the inputs contained sexual and erotic content.

Past work has analyzed porn consumption as a means to study sexual behavior (Hald, 2006; Harvey, 2020). Doing so can evade the limitations of more traditional sexual studies such as experimentation, which demands time-consuming planning to comply with ethical guidelines (Pearson and Curtis, 2025). Like studying porn, analyzing sexual conversations between users and conversational agents may be a viable way to study sexual behavior. Because this type of study doesn't require deploying surveys–the traditional method for studying porn consumption–it may surpass the advantages of studying porn in terms of scalability and ease of study. It also has the added advantage of rich textual data exemplifying the ways people think and talk about sex. This type of sexual experience will be more tailored to the user's particular wants than porn, and therefore potentially more informative to study.

It has long been recognized that, though porn can serve as a safe space for the queer community (Flory, 2024), the representation of LGBTQ+ people in mainstream porn can be problematic (Harvey, 2020). For example, transgender people may be dehumanized by being overly-objectified (Anzani et al., 2021). Lesbian representation in mainstream porn largely caters to the male gaze, leading to fetishization (Smyth, 1990; Collins, 1998; Webber, 2013). Though generally thought of as less problematic, male gay porn has been critiqued for reinforcing homophobia (Corneau and van der Meulen, 2014).

Like porn, erotic conversational agents have their advantages for queer populations, such as providing emotional support (Lissak et al., 2024). However, we seek to understand whether–in spite of these positive effects–problematic representations of LGBTQ+ people observed in porn can also be

Proceedings of the Queer in AI Workshop, pages 17–25

found in user prompts with conversational agents. To this end, the main contributions of this work include: (1) an analysis of the way users represent LGBTQ+ people in sexual interactions with ChatGPT using an extended version of Mendelsohn et al. (2020)'s pre-existing framework for identifying dehumanizing language and (2) a discussion of our findings that motivates further exploration of sexual interactions with LLM-powered conversational agents.

2 Related Work

In this section we cover the background on LLMs and sexuality, discuss NLP for queer sociolinguistics and cover prior dehumanization work.

2.1 LLMs and Sexuality

Erotic conversational agents are increasing in popularity; male and queer audiences are common early adopters (Gesselman et al., 2023). Döring et al. (2024) identified several sexual use-cases for these agents, such as for sexual education and therapy. Other work in this vein has evaluated LLMs' understanding of sexual consent (Marcantonio et al., 2023), sexual medical information (Seyam et al., 2024; Caglar et al., 2023), their ability to act as therapists (D'Souza et al., 2023; Vowels, 2024) and their biases (Organization, 2022; Dhingra et al., 2023; Wan et al., 2023; Kotek et al., 2023). Though many studies focus on the LLM component of these interactions, few have examined the phenomena as a way to understand human sexuality. As Pearson and Curtis (2025) argue, this could be a rich research opportunity (Hald, 2006).

2.2 NLP for Queer Sociolinguistics

Several works have used NLP techniques to analyze linguistic phenomena related to the LGBTQ+ population. Andersen et al. (2024) analyzed the Twitter discourse around the Mexican Spanish-speaking LGBTQ+ community over ten years. By mapping how the polarity of some nouns related to the LGBTQ+ community has evolved in conversational settings, the authors found that, on average, the analyzed tweets had a negative polarity. Furthermore, the authors revealed that the nouns related to the trans community have seen the greatest increase in usage for the time range and subgroups represented in their corpus. Locatelli et al. (2023) performed a cross-lingual analysis of LGBTQ+ discourse on Twitter across seven languages during the 2022 Pride month. Their results indicate that *homotransphobia* is a global problem that takes on distinct cultural expressions. In line with the paper presented by Andersen et al. (2024), Locatelli et al. (2023) found that derogatory language toward LGBTQ+ people is present in the seven languages they studied while being especially prevalent in Italian and French.

2.3 Dehumanization and Language

Haslam (2006) presents two types of dehumanization explored in prior work: animalistic (likening a target group to animals) or mechanistic (treating a target group as machines or inanimate objects). For example, Tutsis in Rwanda were explicitly compared to cockroaches in propaganda leading up to the 1994 genocide (Harris and Fiske, 2011). They propose that these types of dehumanization can also occur in subtler cases in which groups are not sufficiently attributed human qualities. For example, feminist work has discussed dehumanization in porn through the sexual objectification of women (Zhou et al., 2021); these women are stripped of human qualities such as emotionality. Cascalheira and Choi (2023), in their study of dehumanization of transgender people, echo that sexual objectification is an important element of dehumanization and can have negative impact on mental health (Anzani et al., 2021).

Mendelsohn et al. (2020) built on Haslam (2006) to present a computational framework for identifying dehumanizing language. They analyzed mentions of LGBTQ+ individuals in the New York Times over 30 years (1986 to 2015), finding decreasing association of LGBTQ+ groups with dehumanizing elements such as vermin metaphors and moral disgust. Giorgi et al. (2023) used this framework for their analysis of the dehumanization of those who use substances in U.S. news media. Burovova and Romanyshyn (2024) take another approach in their analysis of the dehumanization of Ukrainians on Russian Social Media, using a sentence-level binary classifier to identify dehumanization. To our knowledge, this work is the first to leverage this type of computational framework to examine dehumanization in erotic content.

3 Data

We conduct our analysis on a filtered portion of the WildChat-1M-Full dataset (Zhao et al., 2024),[1]

[1] https://huggingface.co/datasets/allenai/WildChat-1M-Full?not-for-all-audiences=true

which contains 1 million conversations between users and OpenAI's GPT-3.5 and 4. We filter the dataset to only include conversations in English which have been marked by the included OpenAI Moderation results as containing sexual content. Because we are interested in studying how *humans* characterize those from LGBTQ+ communities (rather than how LLMs do), we remove all system responses from the set. The resulting dataset contains approximately 38 thousand unique user turns from sexual conversations.

To identify mentions of various groups, we build a lexicon based on the Textual Identity Detection and Augmentation Lexicon (TIDAL),[2] a dataset formed to enable automatic detection of identity labels (Klu and Sethi, 2023). It has coverage for identity groups including race, nationality, ethnicity, sexual orientation, gender identity, gender expression, sex characteristics and religion; it includes slurs. Because our vector approaches (discussed in Section 4) rely on word embeddings, we only consider single-word nouns. Based on these words, we formed lexicons to identify mentions for seven groups: LGBTQ+, LGB, Transgender, Gay Men, Lesbian, Bisexual, and Heterosexual. Word lists for each group are included in Appendix A.1.

4 Measuring Dehumanization

Mendelsohn et al. (2020) present a structure for analyzing dehumanization in media. They outline several elements of dehumanization from prior social psychology literature including: a) negative evaluation of a target group, b) moral disgust, and c) vermin as a dehumanizing metaphor. We follow their framework for analyzing each element and add an additional component: d) objectification.

(a) Negative Evaluation of a Target Group Prior work shows that negative evaluations of a target group contribute to the dehumanization of the group (Haslam, 2006). To quantify this, we complete a simple per-sentence sentiment analysis with the SiEBERT model (Hartmann et al., 2023).[3] To obtain a sentiment score for each group label, we average over the scores for every sentence containing a term associated with the group.

(b) Moral Disgust To identify moral disgust associated with each group–another indicator of dehumanization–we lean on lexicons created by Graham et al. (2009) for each dimension from Moral Foundations theory (Haidt and Graham, 2007). Specifically, we use all words from the "moral disgust lexicon", which includes about 80 words such as *obscene*, *sin*, and *sick* (see full lexicon in Appendix A.1). We train a word2vec skip-gram model[4] on our dataset to create a moral disgust "concept vector" by averaging the embeddings for all moral disgust words (Mikolov et al., 2013). Then, we measure the cosine distance between this concept vector and concept vectors for all groups. We compare these distances to a "neutral" concept vector, constructed by averaging the embeddings for the words *person*, *people*, *individual*, and *individuals*.

(c) Vermin Metaphor Another way people are dehumanized is when they are robbed of human traits and attributed those of animals such as vermin (Haslam, 2006). To measure the association of different groups with vermin in the dataset, we repeat our method for measuring moral disgust–we create a vermin concept vector by averaging the word embeddings for vermin words (*vermin*, *rodent(s)*, *rat(s)*, *mice*, *cockroach(es)*) and measure cosine distance between this vector and the concept vectors for the group labels.

(d) Objectification Haslam (2006) discusses mechanistic dehumanization, or treating a target as an inanimate object. This is related to sexual objectification, and thus pertinent to our analysis. We measure the association of different groups with objects in the dataset. We repeat our method for measuring vermin metaphor and moral disgust–we create an object concept vector by averaging the word embeddings for "object" words including *it*, *that*, *this*, *thing*, *things*, *object*, *objects*, *item*, *items*, *machine*, and *machines*. Then we measure the cosine distance between this and the group concept vectors.

5 Dehumanization of LGBTQ+ People in Wildchat

In our analysis of the dehumanization of LGBTQ+ people in user prompts in the sexual subset of the Wildchat dataset, we unveil a number of interesting insights which point to diverse portrayals of

[2] https://github.com/google-research-datasets/TIDAL

[3] https://huggingface.co/siebert/sentiment-roberta-large-english

[4] https://radimrehurek.com/gensim/models/word2vec.html

LGBTQ+ groups in human interactions with LLM-powered agents.

LGBTQ+ people are objectified less than "neutral" terms. In Figure 1, we find evidence that LGBTQ+ terms are used in less similar contexts to object words than the predetermined "neutral" terms. The Vermin Metaphor results (shown in Figure 6), show that *all* LGBTQ+ word groupsw are, on average, used in less similar context to vermin words than the "neutral" terms. In Figure 7, we find that some of the group vectors have a smaller cosine distance to the "Moral Disgust" concept vector, while others (including "Bisexual" and "Gay Men") have slightly longer distances. Collectively, these results seem to indicate that these groups are characterized with similar levels of, or less, dehumanizing language than the terms *person*, *people*, *individual*, and *individuals*.

Dehumanization is relatively similar across groups. The "vermin", "object", and "moral disgust" vectors exhibit similar cosine distances to the vectors associated with each subgroup in the LGBTQ+ acronym. While some groups may be dehumanized more, the differences are not stark. This indicates that on average, when people ask ChatGPT to generate text with LGBTQ+-related erotic content, they tend to dehumanize every subgroup in a similar measure.

However, some terms, such as "twink" and "faggot", exhibit the longest cosine distance from the moral disgust concept vector when compared to all the other terms in the LGBTQ+ category, indicating a semantic shift in these terms. One possible reason for this is that societal acceptance of gay men has led some ChatGPT users to view them in a more positive and sexually desirable way. The same cannot be said for other LGBTQ+ groups.

Transgender and lesbian populations are dehumanized more than other groups. In line with patterns in mainstream porn, we find that lesbian and transgender people are stripped of human qualities more often than other groups. In Figure 7 we observe that the "Transgender" group vector is more closely related to the moral disgust concept vector than any other group vector. The "Lesbian" group vector is also situated nearer the "moral disgust" concept vector than the "neutral" vector. These groups also face more negative evaluations, as shown in Figure 2.

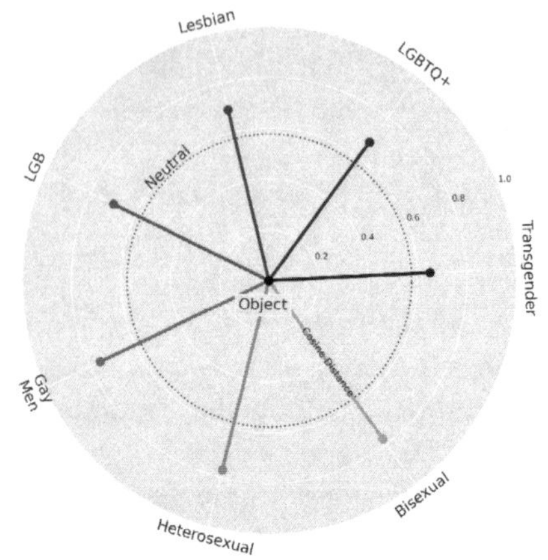

Figure 1: Cosine distance from Object Concept Vector to each subgroup. An average distance over all terms in the category is shown.

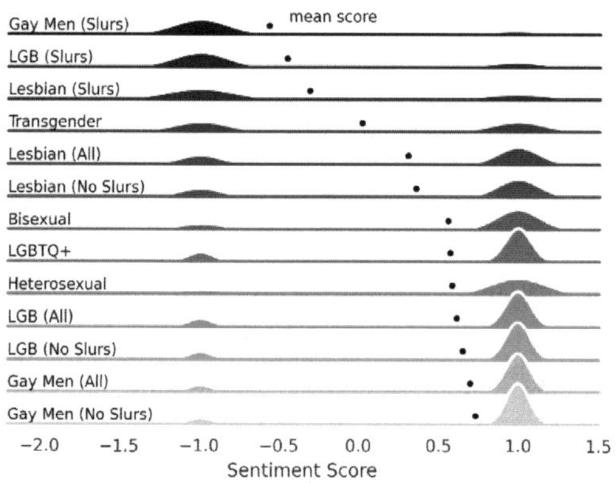

Figure 2: Distribution of sentiment scores for each group. Mean score is calculated over the sentiment labels for sentences containing a term in the group.

Outdated terms are used in more dehumanizing contexts. In line with Mendelsohn et al. (2020)'s findings in their analysis of dehumanization in U.S. news media, outdated terms used to refer to people from the LGBTQ+ community are used in more dehumanizing ways than other terms, such. For example, the terms "homosexual" and "hermaphrodite" are generally considered to be outdated and offensive.[5]. These words are more closely associated with the vermin, object, and moral disgust concept vectors than other LGBTQ+ terms (Figures 3, 4, and 8).

Some interactions represent LGBTQ+ people in more positive ways. Finally, we remark that the various concept vectors we model here–which

[5]https://glaad.org/reference/terms/

Term(s)	User Prompt	Dehumanization
Twinks	The twinks and Shrek are relaxing in bed au naturel and snacking on roasted fish (that died from Shrek farting in a pond during his morning bath with the twinks, and he later cooked up for them) as they chat while Shrek couples with one of them (describe Shrek's physique and butt).	Some
Lesbian	She very slowly begins to realize she is attracted to girls, at first denying it, but very slowly accepting that she is a lesbian and eventually finds a girlfriend named Lola who is just like her, physically and mentally, and they begin dating, and after months of dating, on a date while walking through the park, she got on one knee and proposed, to which her girlfriend immedietly responded with a yes.	No
Lesbian, Hetero	Write a chapter of 1000 words about a hot lesbian couple that love to do lesbian acts in front of hetero men.	Yes

Table 1: Selected examples of terms in user prompts.

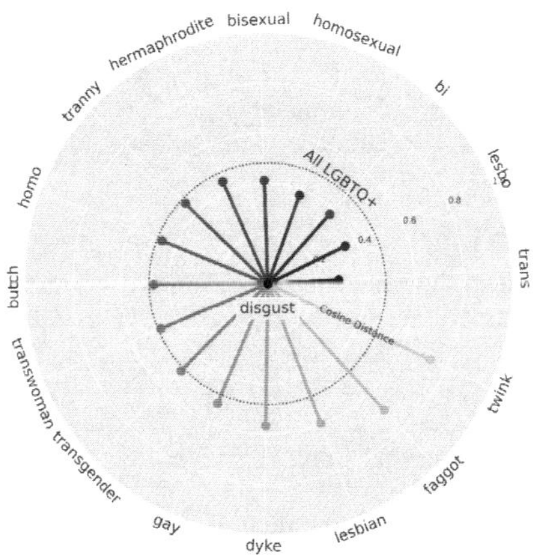

Figure 3: Cosine distance from the Moral Disgust vector to the vector of terms in the LGBTQ+ category.

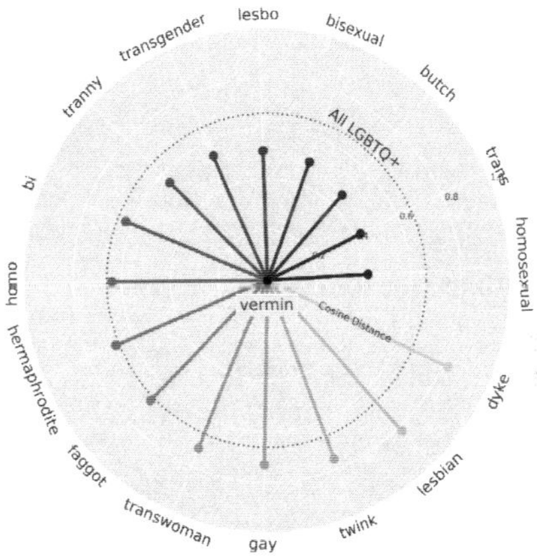

Figure 4: Cosine distance from the Vermin vector to the vector of terms in the LGBTQ+ category.

reveal dehumanizing language targeted at the LGBTQ+ population–indicate that not all interactions are dehumanizing LGBTQ+ people. This is further evidenced by some of the selected examples included in Table 1.

As a result, our analysis does not yield one single, binary conclusion about the ways in which LGBTQ+ are being characterized by users in interactions with AI-powered agents. Rather, it reinforces that the conversation around sexual interactions with these agents, much like around porn, must remain complex and nuanced. Though we find evidence of dehumanizing language in our quantitative and qualitative analysis–which seems to mirror the demand for this type of content in mainstream porn (Anzani et al., 2021; Webber, 2013)–we also find content that is more uplifting. We suggest that this *could* be further evidence that these agents are helpful tools actively being used by those who cannot find proper representation of their desires in mainstream media (Gesselman et al., 2023).

6 Conclusion

Motivated by our findings, we call attention to further studying how conversational agents facilitate or hinder marginalized groups' representation in sexual contexts. We propose extending this work to explore representation across lines of race and gender. Our findings also suggest that it may be informative to expand our focus past dehumanizing language to study other possible modes of representation.

By understanding how people reproduce harmful stereotypes–or not–in their prompting practices of erotic text, we could develop safeguards to minimize the dehumanization of the LGBTQ+ community, while promoting the use of these tools among LGBTQ+ individuals who cannot find proper representation of their desires in traditional media.

7 Limitations

The findings reported in this paper are based on a subset of human-generated ChatGPT prompts.

Therefore, claiming that these can be generalized to every interaction with every commercial LLM is inaccurate. Further analyses with data gathered from a longer timespan and multiple LLMs could support or refute the claims we report here. Furthermore, given the time and computational constraints, we limit our studies to only a subset of the original WildChat-1M-Full dataset.

Another noteworthy limitation of this work is the language diversity in our data. We limited our experiments to prompts written in English, ignoring the existing epistemic diversity in human-agent interactions.

We also acknowledge the tendency of automatic sentiment analysis to ignore in-group mentions of slurs. Therefore, the sentiment scores may be negatively biased when slurs are present.

References

Scott Andersen, Segio-Luis Ojeda-Trueba, Juan Vásquez, and Gemma Bel-Enguix. 2024. The Mexican gayze: A computational analysis of the attitudes towards the LGBT+ population in Mexico on social media across a decade. In *Proceedings of the 8th Workshop on Online Abuse and Harms (WOAH 2024)*, pages 178–200, Mexico City, Mexico. Association for Computational Linguistics.

Annalisa Anzani, Louis Lindley, Giacomo Tognasso, M. Paz Galupo, and Antonio Prunas. 2021. "being talked to like i was a sex toy, like being transgender was simply for the enjoyment of someone else": Fetishization and sexualization of transgender and nonbinary individuals. *Archives of Sexual Behavior*, 50(3):897–911.

Kateryna Burovova and Mariana Romanyshyn. 2024. Computational analysis of dehumanization of ukrainians on Russian social media. In *Proceedings of the 8th Joint SIGHUM Workshop on Computational Linguistics for Cultural Heritage, Social Sciences, Humanities and Literature (LaTeCH-CLfL 2024)*, pages 28–39, St. Julians, Malta. Association for Computational Linguistics.

U. Caglar, O. Yildiz, M. F. Ozervarli, R. Aydin, O. Sarilar, F. Ozgor, and M. Ortac. 2023. Assessing the performance of chat generative pretrained transformer (chatgpt) in answering andrology-related questions. *Urology research & practice*, 49(6).

Cory Jacob Cascalheira and Na-Yeun Choi. 2023. Transgender dehumanization and mental health: Microaggressions, sexual objectification, and shame. *The Counseling Psychologist*, 51(4):532–559.

Dana Collins. 1998. Lesbian pornographic production: Creating social/cultural space for subverting representations of sexuality. *Berkeley Journal of Sociology*, 43:31–62.

Simon Corneau and Emily van der Meulen. 2014. Some like it mellow: On gay men complicating pornography discourses. *Journal of Homosexuality*, 61(4):491–510. PMID: 24245563.

Harnoor Dhingra, Preetiha Jayashanker, Sayali Moghe, and Emma Strubell. 2023. Queer people are people first: Deconstructing sexual identity stereotypes in large language models.

Nicola Döring, Thuy Dung Le, Laura Vowels, Matthew Vowels, and Tiffany Marcantonio. 2024. The impact of artificial intelligence on human sexuality: A five-year literature review 2020–2024. *Current Sexual Health Reports*, 17:1–39.

Russell Franco D'Souza, Shabbir Amanullah, Mary Mathew, and Krishna Mohan Surapaneni. 2023. Appraising the performance of chatgpt in psychiatry using 100 clinical case vignettes. *Asian Journal of Psychiatry*, 89:103770.

Isabelle Marie Flory. 2024. Porn is blunt [...] i had way more lgbtq+ friendly education through porn: The experiences of lgbtq+ individuals with online pornography. *Sexualities*.

Amanda N. Gesselman, Ellen M. Kaufman, Alexandra S. Marcotte, Tania A. Reynolds, and Justin R. Garcia. 2023. Engagement with emerging forms of sextech: Demographic correlates from a national sample of adults in the united states. *The Journal of Sex Research*, 60(2):177–189. PMID: 35104185.

Salvatore Giorgi, Daniel Roy Sadek Habib, Douglas Bellew, Garrick Sherman, and Brenda Curtis. 2023. A linguistic analysis of dehumanization toward substance use across three decades of news articles. *Frontiers in Public Health*, 11.

Jesse Graham, Jonathan Haidt, and Brian A. Nosek. 2009. Liberals and conservatives rely on different sets of moral foundations. *Journal of Personality and Social Psychology*, 96(5):1029–1046.

Paolo Grigis and Antonella De Angeli. 2024. Roleplay with large language model-based characters: A creative writers perspective (short paper) paolo grigis. In *SYNERGY@AVI*.

Jonathan Haidt and Jesse Graham. 2007. When morality opposes justice: Conservatives have moral intuitions that liberals may not recognize. *Social Justice Research*, 20(1):98–116.

Gert Martin Hald. 2006. Gender differences in pornography consumption among young heterosexual danish adults. *Archives of Sexual Behavior*, 35(5):577–585.

Lasana T. Harris and Susan T. Fiske. 2011. Dehumanized perception a psychological means to facilitate atrocities, torture, and genocide? *Zeitschrift fur Psychologie / Journal of Psychology*, 219(3):175–181.

Jochen Hartmann, Mark Heitmann, Christian Siebert, and Christina Schamp. 2023. More than a feeling: Accuracy and application of sentiment analysis. *International Journal of Research in Marketing*, 40(1):75–87.

Penny Harvey. 2020. *Let's Talk About Porn: The Perceived Effect of Online Mainstream Pornography on LGBTQ Youth*, page 31–52. Springer International Publishing, Cham.

Nick Haslam. 2006. Dehumanization: An integrative review. *Personality and Social Psychology Review*, 10(3):252–264.

Emmanuel Klu and Sameer Sethi. 2023. Tide: Textual identity detection for evaluating and augmenting classification and language models. *Preprint*, arXiv:2309.04027.

Hadas Kotek, Rikker Dockum, and David Sun. 2023. Gender bias and stereotypes in large language models. In *Proceedings of The ACM Collective Intelligence Conference*, CI '23, page 12–24, New York, NY, USA. Association for Computing Machinery.

Weixin Liang, Yaohui Zhang, Zhengxuan Wu, Haley Lepp, Wenlong Ji, Xuandong Zhao, Hancheng Cao, Sheng Liu, Siyu He, Zhi Huang, Diyi Yang, Christopher Potts, Christopher D Manning, and James Y. Zou. 2024. Mapping the increasing use of llms in scientific papers.

Shir Lissak, Nitay Calderon, Geva Shenkman, Yaakov Ophir, Eyal Fruchter, Anat Brunstein Klomek, and Roi Reichart. 2024. The colorful future of LLMs: Evaluating and improving LLMs as emotional supporters for queer youth. In *Proceedings of the 2024 Conference of the North American Chapter of the Association for Computational Linguistics: Human Language Technologies (Volume 1: Long Papers)*, pages 2040–2079, Mexico City, Mexico. Association for Computational Linguistics.

Davide Locatelli, Greta Damo, and Debora Nozza. 2023. A cross-lingual study of homotransphobia on twitter. In *Proceedings of the First Workshop on Cross-Cultural Considerations in NLP (C3NLP)*, pages 16–24.

Tiffany L. Marcantonio, Michelle Haikalis Karen E. Nielsen, Ruschelle M. Leone, Jacqueline Woerner, Elizabeth C. Neilson, and Anne Marie Schipani-McLaughlin. 2023. Hey chatgpt, let's talk about sexual consent. *The Journal of Sex Research*, 0(0):1–12. PMID: 37707442.

Julia Mendelsohn, Yulia Tsvetkov, and Dan Jurafsky. 2020. A Framework for the Computational Linguistic Analysis of Dehumanization. *Frontiers in Artificial Intelligence*, 3:55.

Tomas Mikolov, Ilya Sutskever, Kai Chen, Greg Corrado, and Jeffrey Dean. 2013. Distributed representations of words and phrases and their compositionality. *Preprint*, arXiv:1310.4546.

Niloofar Mireshghallah, Maria Antoniak, Yash More, Yejin Choi, and G. Farnadi. 2024. Trust no bot: Discovering personal disclosures in human-llm conversations in the wild. *arXiv*, abs/2407.11438.

Subigya Nepal, Arvind Pillai, William Campbell, Talie Massachi, Michael V. Heinz, Ashmita Kunwar, Eunsol Soul Choi, Xuhai Xu, Joanna Kuc, Jeremy F. Huckins, Jason Holden, Sarah M. Preum, Colin Depp, Nicholas Jacobson, Mary P. Czerwinski, Eric Granholm, and Andrew T. Campbell. 2024. Mindscape study: Integrating llm and behavioral sensing for personalized ai-driven journaling experiences. *Proc. ACM Interact. Mob. Wearable Ubiquitous Technol.*, 8(4).

World Health Organization. 2022. *Ageism in artificial intelligence for health: WHO policy brief.* World Health Organization.

Samuel Pearson and Caitlin Curtis. 2025. Erotic ai chatbots offer research opportunities for the behavioral sciences. *Archives of Sexual Behavior*.

R M Seyam, B S Khan, S A Aljazaeri, T Z Arabi, S S Alkhateeb, M F Alotaibi, and W M Altaweel. 2024. Artificial Intelligence ChatGPT and GPT4 Performance on Male and Female Sexual Dysfunction, Sexually Transmitted Infection, and Male Factor Infertility in the 2019 to 2023 American Urological Association Self-Assessment Study Programs. *The Journal of Sexual Medicine*, 21:qdae002.033.

Cherry Smyth. 1990. The pleasure threshold: Looking at lesbian pornography on film. *Feminist Review*, 34(1).

Laura M. Vowels. 2024. Are chatbots the new relationship experts? insights from three studies. *Computers in Human Behavior: Artificial Humans*, 2(2):100077.

Yixin Wan, George Pu, Jiao Sun, Aparna Garimella, Kai-Wei Chang, and Nanyun Peng. 2023. "kelly is a warm person, joseph is a role model": Gender biases in LLM-generated reference letters.

Valerie Webber. 2013. Shades of gay: Performance of girl-on-girl pornography and mobile authenticities. *Sexualities*, 16(1-2).

Wenting Zhao, Xiang Ren, Jack Hessel, Claire Cardie, Yejin Choi, and Yuntian Deng. 2024. Wildchat: 1m chatGPT interaction logs in the wild. In *The Twelfth International Conference on Learning Representations*.

Xuhui Zhou, Zhe Su, Tiwalayo Eisape, Hyunwoo Kim, and Maarten Sap. 2024. Is this the real life? is this just fantasy? the misleading success of simulating social interactions with LLMs.

Yanyan Zhou, (Harry) Yaojun Yan, Tuo Liu, and Paul Bryant. 2021. Pornography use, two forms of dehumanization, and sexual aggression: Attitudes vs. behaviors. *Journal of Sex & Marital Therapy*, 47(6):571–590.

A Appendix

A.1 Lexicons

Vermin *vermin, rodent, rodents, rat, rats, mice, cockroach, cockroaches, termite, termites, bedbug, bedbugs, fleas*

Moral Disgust *disgust*, deprav*, disease*, unclean*, contagio*, indecen*, sin, sinful*, sinner*, sins, sinned, sinning, slut*, whore, dirt*, impiety, impious, profan*, gross, repuls*, sick*, promiscu*, lewd*, adulter*, debauche* , defile*, tramp, prostitut*, unchaste, intemperate, wanton, profligate, filth* , trashy, obscen*, lax, taint*, stain*, tarnish*, debase*, desecrat*, wicked*, blemish, exploitat*, pervert, wretched**

Neutral *person, people, individual, individuals*

Object *it, that, this, thing, things, object, objects, item, items, machine, machines*

Groups

LGBTQ+ *lgbt, lgbtq, lgbtqs, lgbts, bisexual, bisexuals, gay, gays, homosexual, homosexuals, lesbian, lesbians, ftm, ftms, mtf, mtfs, trans, transes, transgender, transgenders, hermaphrodite, hermaphrodites, trannies, tranny, transexual, transexuals, transman, transmen, transwoman, transwomen, transsexual, transsexuals, pansexual, pansexuals, nonbinaries, nonbinary, bi, bis, butch, butches, dyke, dykes, faggot, faggots, homo, homos, lesbo, lesbos, lgbtqia, lgbtqias, poly, polys, twink, twinks*

LGB *bisexual, bisexuals, gay, gays, faggot, faggots, homo, homos, twink, twinks, homosexual, homosexuals, lesbian, lesbians, butch, butches, dyke, dykes, lesbo, lesbos*

Transgender *ftm, ftms, mtf, mtfs, trans, transes, transgender, transgenders, hermaphrodite, hermaphrodites, trannies, tranny, transman, transmen, transwoman, transwomen*

Gay Men *gay, gays, faggot, faggots, homo, homos, twink, twinks*

Lesbian *lesbian, lesbians, butch, butches, dyke, dykes, lesbo, lesbos*

Bisexual *bi, bis, bisexual, bisexuals*

Heterosexual *hetero, heteros, heterosexual, heterosexuals*

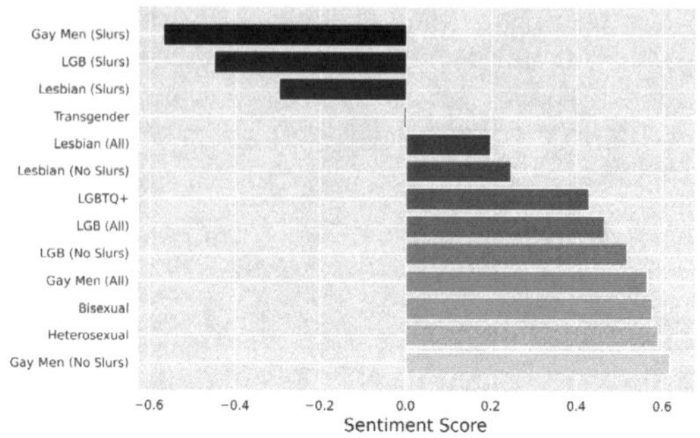

Figure 5: Sentiment score for each group. The score is calculated by taking an average over the sentiment labels (-1 for negative and 1 for positive) for all sentences containing a term in the group category.

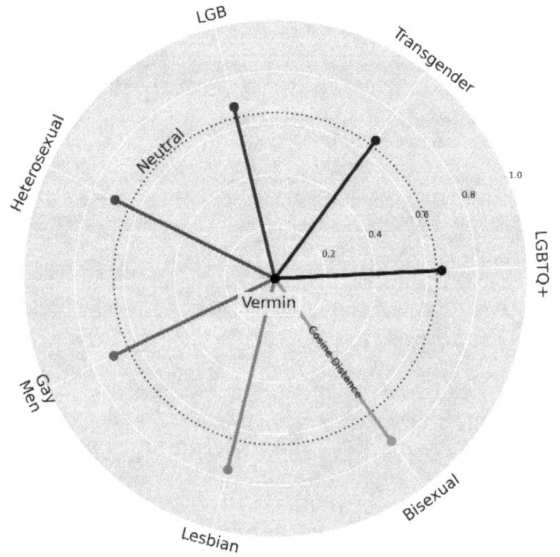

Figure 6: Cosine distance from Vermin Concept Vector to each subgroup. Subgroup distance is calculated by averaging over the distance of each term in the subgroup to the concept vector.

B Additional Tables and Plots

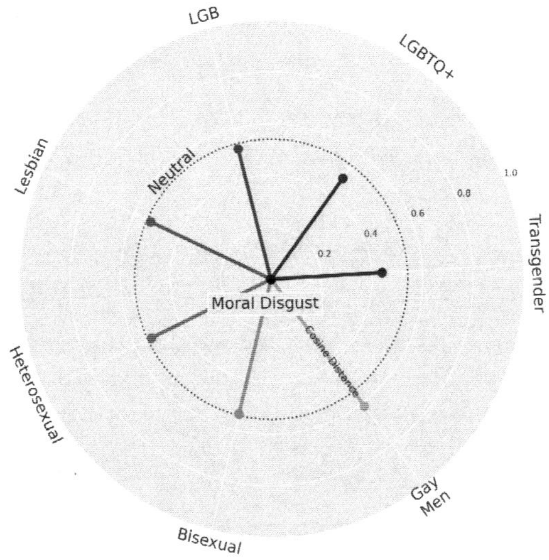

Figure 7: Cosine distance from Moral Disgust Concept Vector to each subgroup. Subgroup distance is calculated by averaging over the distance of each term in the subgroup to the concept vector.

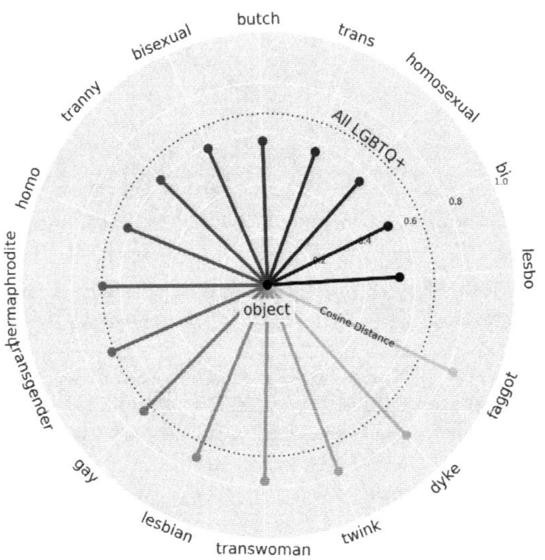

Figure 8: Cosine distance from Object Concept Vector to each term in the LGBTQ+ category. An average distance over all terms in the category is shown.

Leveraging Large Language Models in Detecting Anti-LGBTQIA+ User-generated Texts

Quoc-Toan Nguyen[1], **Josh Nguyen**[2], **Van-Tuan Pham**[3], **William John Teahan**[4]

[1]*University of Technology Sydney,* [2]*The University of Melbourne,*
[3]*RMIT University,* [4]*Bangor University*

✉Corresponding Author: w.j.teahan@bangor.ac.uk

Abstract

Anti-LGBTQIA+ texts in user-generated content pose significant risks to online safety and inclusivity. This study investigates the capabilities and limitations of five widely adopted Large Language Models (LLMs)—DeepSeek-V3, GPT-4o, GPT-4o-mini, GPT-o1-mini, and Llama3.3-70B—in detecting such harmful content. Our findings reveal that while LLMs demonstrate potential in identifying offensive language, their effectiveness varies across models and metrics, with notable shortcomings in calibration. Furthermore, linguistic analysis exposes deeply embedded patterns of discrimination, reinforcing the urgency for improved detection mechanisms for this marginalised population. In summary, this study demonstrates the significant potential of LLMs for practical application in detecting anti-LGBTQIA+ user-generated texts and provides valuable insights from text analysis that can inform topic modelling. These findings contribute to developing safer digital platforms and enhancing protection for LGBTQIA+ individuals.

⚠Warning: Given the research's objectives, this paper includes profanity, vulgarity, and other harmful language. These may be disturbing for queer or LGBTQIA+ individuals and other readers.

1 Introduction

The dramatic growth of user-generated content (Gorwa et al., 2020) underscores the urgent need to prevent the spread of intentionally and unintentionally harmful material across Online Social Networks (OSNs) or other digital platforms. Initially, user-generated text moderation relied on manual, rule-based methods, but with advancements in Artificial Intelligence (AI), OSNs and digital platforms have increasingly applied advanced technologies to uphold platform integrity. These developments are essential to protect both users and online communities from harmful content (Franco et al., 2024).

Abusive language or cyberbullying are among the most vital problems, and continue to pose significant challenges worldwide, affecting a vast number of individuals (Hong et al., 2025). If left unaddressed, such harmful interactions can greatly heighten the risk of suicidal thoughts and behaviours (Gini and Espelage, 2014). Although the relationship between bullying and suicidality—including suicidal ideation and attempts—is complex, research strongly indicates that victimization plays a major role in increasing this risk, often leading to severe psychological consequences for those affected (Holt et al., 2015). A promising approach to mitigating this problem is the development of AI-based moderation systems (Cedric et al., 2022; Todor et al., 2023; Calabrese et al., 2024), which can efficiently detect abusive language on a large scale. Especially, utilising **Large Language Models (LLMs)** has notably advanced this task (Neele et al., 2024; Sarah et al., 2024; Prince et al., 2024; Franco et al., 2024; Wei et al., 2024; Hyundong et al., 2024).

However, the previous studies typically adopt a universal framework neglecting the evaluation and specific development, leading to high potential risks for queer individuals (Jordan et al., 2024) or LGBTQIA+ community (Are et al., 2024) [1] despite growing evidence that they experience cyberbullying at significantly higher rates and at significantly higher rates than their heterosexual peers (Oliver et al., 2021; Abreu and Kenny, 2018). Cyberbullying among LGBTQIA+ individuals has been linked to a wide range of harmful consequences (Abreu and Kenny, 2018), including severe psychological and emotional distress such as depression, low self-esteem, and an increased risk of suicidal thoughts and attempts. Furthermore, it can also contribute

[1]LGBTQIA+ stands for lesbian, gay, bisexual, transgender, queer or questioning, intersex, and asexual. The "+" symbol includes other identities that may not be explicitly listed in the acronym.

Proceedings of the Queer in AI Workshop, pages 26–34
May 4, 2025 ©2025 Association for Computational Linguistics

to behavioural issues, such as heightened physical aggression, body image concerns, and social isolation (Abreu and Kenny, 2018). Therefore, when leveraging LLMs for user-generated text moderation on OSNs or other digital platforms (websites, mobile apps,...), it is crucial to assess their effectiveness in identifying harmful or anti-LGBTQIA+ user-generated text (Schey and Shelton, 2023) before deployment. Without proper evaluation, LLMs may fail to recognize subtle forms of discrimination, reinforce biases, or even inadvertently allow harmful user-generated texts to persist, ultimately exacerbating the challenges faced by people in the LGBTQIA+ community.

Hence, in this paper, we leverage five LLMs including DeepSeek-V3 (Liu et al., 2024), GPT-4o (Hurst et al., 2024), GPT-4o mini (Hurst et al., 2024), GPT-o1-mini (Aaron et al., 2024), and Llama3.3-70b (Jonas et al., 2025) which are among the most widely-used and up-to-date methods in the literature, to answer the following Research Questions (RQs) using user-generated texts comments data from YouTube, Reddit, and X with anti-LGBTQIA+ user-generated content (Pratik et al., 2022):

- **RQ1**: What are the predominant linguistic patterns and strongest associations in anti-LGBTQIA+ user-generated texts?
- **RQ2**: How can we leverage LLMs to detect anti-LGBTQIA+ user-generated texts?
- **RQ3**: How effectively do LLMs detect anti-LGBTQIA+ user-generated texts, and how do their predictive performance and calibration differ in this task?

2 Related Work

Recent studies highlight the growing role of LLMs in automated content moderation. Sarah et al. (2024) proved LLMs' contextual understanding aids hate speech detection. Neele et al. (2024) proved the potential of user-driven moderation but pointed out scalability challenges. Wei et al. (2024) demonstrated that LLM pipelines reduce computational costs while maintaining high accuracy. Cedric et al. (2022) emphasized detecting minority arguments for better understanding in debates. Franco et al. (2024) highlighted LLMs' support in moderation dynamics, though reasoning limitations remain. Kou and Gui (2020) stressed the importance of community-aligned explanations in AI-led moderation.

Nevertheless, existing research predominantly addresses the general population, with limited evaluation of these methods specifically for the LGBTQIA+ community. This gap raises concerns regarding potential biases and shortcomings that may disproportionately affect this marginalised group. However, studies addressing this issue remain limited in the literature. While LLMs have shown advancements over conventional AI models, current methodologies for anti-LGBTQIA+ user-generated content still primarily rely on conventional AI approaches (Vivek et al., 2024; Arora et al., 2024).

3 Methods

3.1 Material

This study utilises a part of a dataset by Pratik et al. (2022) comprising social media comments collected from various users on YouTube, Reddit, and X (formerly known as Twitter). They were labelled by 11143 annotators recruited via Amazon Mechanical Turk. 4299 samples are manually selected and labelled from the original dataset, specifically focusing on content relevant to anti-LGBTQIA+ research following these references' approaches of how to curate the data (J et al., 2024). The data is published by Patel (2025).

We categorise the dataset into two groups: non-anti-LGBTQIA+ and anti-LGBTQIA+. In its raw form, the non-anti-LGBTQIA+ category contains 109764 words, 9634 unique words, while the anti-LGBTQIA+ category comprises 21157 words, with 4023 unique words. After applying common stop words removal, as per (Nothman et al., 2018), the word count for non-anti-LGBTQIA+ is reduced to 50243 words with 9471 unique words (3043 samples), whereas the anti-LGBTQIA+ category retains 11072 words with 3867 unique words (1256 samples). This preprocessing step may refine the dataset for further text analysis. Figure 1 presents examples from both classes.

3.2 User-generated Anti-LGBTQIA+ Text Detection using Large Language Models

Figure 2 illustrates our workflow, demonstrating how LLMs are leveraged for anti-LGBTQIA+ text detection using an example user, x. The process begins when user x sends a text input, denoted as x_{text}. This input is then incorporated into a

Non-anti-LGBTQIA+

- The trans women reading this tweet right now is beautiful
- Sounds like the kinda wholesome life I'd die for never met any black Lesbians before so i guess you're my first ever.
- I met my first gay person, one of my brother's friends, when I was 14. I remained deeply invested in my Methodist faith until I was about 17. I knew the rule—'Man shall not lie with man'—but Jesus also taught to love everyone. So, I wrestled with the question.
- I never switched to bi because of pressure. But I just wanted to leave some happiness in your comments. Don't feel pressured to change just to make things easier for others. Identify as whatever makes you happy and comfy. You're awesome, so be your awesome self! That way you'll be happy and spread your happiness to all of your loved ones.

Anti-LGBTQIA+

- Imagine unironically watching that braindead tranny.
- Quit fucking being an ableist you faggot. Anger issues can't just be dealt with. Kill yourself you pot smoking brain dead one-celled amoeba. Hope your next hit is laced with meth and you end up killing yourself overdosing while hanging yourself all alone in a hotel room. Fucking poser ass retard.
- Women football is trash .. Rapinoe is a filthy lesbian .. Tel her to repent
- And I don't care if you're gay, as long as you aren't a FILTHY CUMSUCKING FAGGOT about it. There is a difference. Don't make being gay your ENTIRE EXISTENCE, and constantly talk about your sex life as if that's the sum of who you are as a person. Not everyone who doesn't agree with homosexual is am evil bigot who wants to herd you all into death camps and electrocute you into being straight.

Figure 1: Examples of user-generated texts from the dataset within the two classes.

developed prompt as x_{input}.

In this prompt, we utilise a "zero-shot" approach (Li et al., 2024; Pengyue et al., 2024; Chi et al., 2024). It is a technique in Natural Language Processing (NLP) where a model performs a task without being provided with specific examples related to that task (Tom et al., 2020; Ross et al., 2023; Hu et al., 2024). Rather than learning from explicit demonstrations, the model relies on a direct task description within the prompt, utilising its pretrained knowledge and reasoning abilities to generate an appropriate response. This approach enables models to adapt to various tasks without requiring additional fine-tuning.

In this prompt, various LLMs—DeepSeek-V3 (Liu et al., 2024), GPT-4o (Hurst et al., 2024), GPT-4o mini (Hurst et al., 2024), GPT-o1-mini (Aaron et al., 2024), and Llama3.3-70b (Jonas et al., 2025)—is leveraged to function as moderator(s) to analyse the given text. Each model represented as F, processes x_{input} to provide an output, denoted as y_{output}, determining whether the text is classified as anti-LGBTQIA+. Additionally, the model provides a score, c, indicating the confidence of its prediction following this black-box approach, asking the confidence score directly from the prompts (Youliang et al., 2024).

For the LLMs' evaluation, multiple samples from various users—denoted as $(x_{\text{text}}^{(1)}, x_{\text{text}}^{(2)}, \ldots, x_{\text{text}}^{(N)})$—are collected from the material described in Section 3.1. Each sample is sequentially processed by the LLMs, including DeepSeek-V3 (Liu et al., 2024), GPT-4o (Hurst et al., 2024), GPT-4o mini (Hurst et al., 2024), GPT-o1-mini (Aaron et al., 2024), and Llama3.3-70b (Jonas et al., 2025). Each sample has an individual classification result y and confidence score c. The final evaluation aggregates the results across all processed samples, ensuring a comprehensive assessment of model performance. The entire workflow for anti-LGBTQIA+ text detection using LLMs can be summarised mathematically as:

$$Y = F(X) = \{(y_i, c_i) \mid y_i, c_i = F_j(x_i), \forall x_i \in X, \forall F_j \in \mathcal{F}\}$$

where:

- $X = \{x_{\text{text}}^{(1)}, x_{\text{text}}^{(2)}, \ldots, x_{\text{text}}^{(N)}\}$ represents the set of user text inputs.
- F_j is an LLM from the set of models:

  $$\mathcal{F} = \{\text{DeepSeek-V3}, \text{Llama3.3-70b}, \text{GPT-4o}, \text{GPT-4o mini}, \text{GPT-o1-mini}\}$$

- Each model F_j takes an input x_i (transformed into $x_{\text{input}}^{(i)}$ through prompting) and outputs:
  - $y_i \in \{0, 1\}$, where 1 indicates the text is classified as anti-LGBTQIA+ and 0 otherwise.
  - $c_i \in [0, 1]$, the confidence score of the classification.

4 Experiments

The experiments of LLMs in this research are completed via model APIs provided by Open AI (OpenAI, 2025) (GPT-4o (Hurst et al., 2024), GPT-4o mini (Hurst et al., 2024), and GPT-o1-mini (Aaron et al., 2024)), and Meta Llama (Meta, 2025) (Llama3.3-70b (Jonas et al., 2025), DeepSeek-V3 (Liu et al., 2024)). The default hyperparameters are set, including `temperature=1.0`, `Top_p=1.0`, and `presence_penalty=0.0`.

In text analysis, a word cloud (Jin, 2017) is used to visualize the top 30 most frequent words in anti-LGBTQIA+ user-generated texts. Additionally, the strongest associations between commonly occurring offensive terms are analysed and visualised by

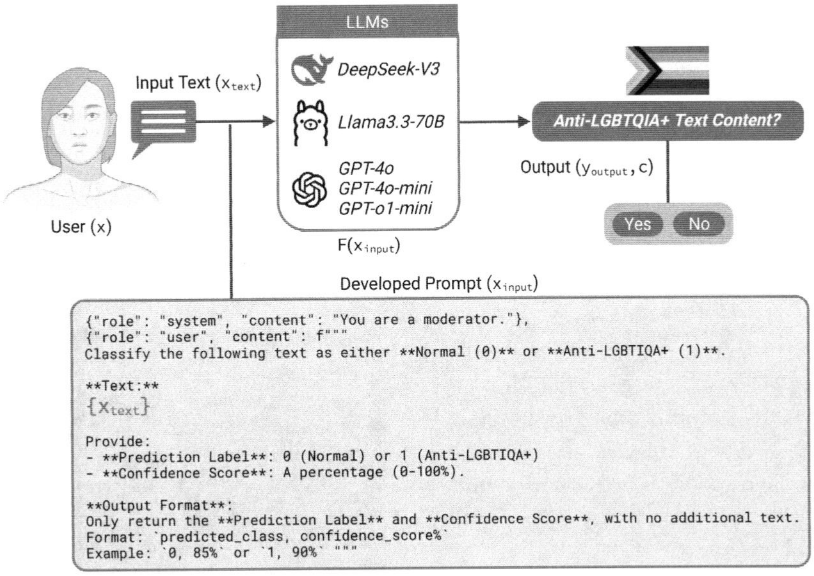

Figure 2: Workflow of the method used for leveraging Large Language Models (LLMs) for user-generated anti-LGBTQIA+ text detection.

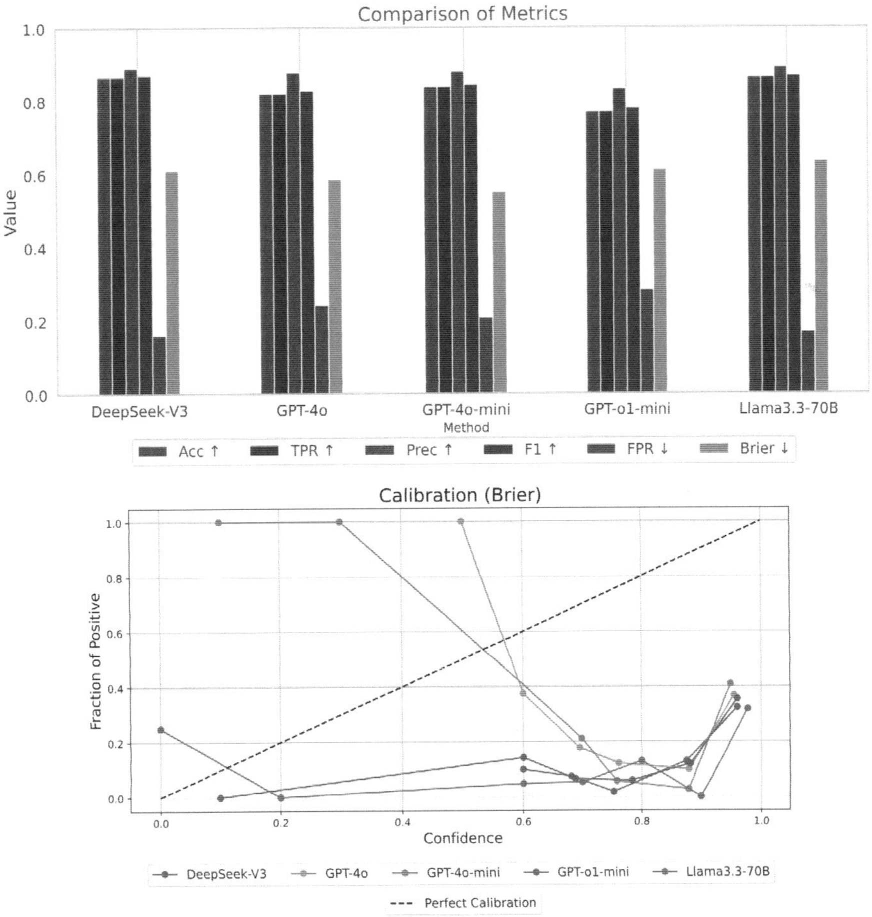

Figure 3: Performance of Large Language Models (LLMs) with metrics. Accuracy ($Acc \uparrow$), True Positive Rate ($TPR \uparrow$), Precision ($Prec \uparrow$), F1-score ($F1 \uparrow$), False Positive Rate ($FPR \downarrow$) and Brier score ($Brier \downarrow$).

a bigram network graph, which visualizes the top 30 most frequent bigrams, using a library named Networkx (Hagberg and Conway, 2020).

Regarding evaluation metrics, five key performance indicators are utilised, each playing a crucial role in AI applications (Hicks et al., 2022). These metrics include **Accuracy** ($Acc \uparrow$), **True Positive Rate** ($TPR \uparrow$), **False Positive Rate** ($FPR \downarrow$), **Precision** ($Prec \uparrow$), and **F1-score** ($F1 \uparrow$). Additionally, the Brier score ($Brier \downarrow$) (Rufibach, 2010) is incorporated as a metric of probabilistic calibration (Youliang et al., 2024). The values for TPR, FPR, Prec, and F1 are computed using macro-averaging. These metrics range from 0 to 1, where **higher values correspond to better performance** for all metrics, except for FPR and $Brier$, where a **better model has lower values**.

5 Results

Word Frequency			Association Frequency	
Word	**Percentage**	**Count**	**Association**	**Count**
faggot	3.775	418	('fucking', 'faggot')	33
fuck	1.933	214	('suck', 'dick')	24
fucking	1.852	205	('fuck', 'faggot')	23
gay	1.581	175	('shut', 'fuck')	21
ass	1.228	136	('faggot', 'ass')	18
faggots	1.030	114	('piece', 'shit')	18
shit	1.021	113	('gon', 'na')	16
fag	0.939	104	('wan', 'na')	13
bitch	0.912	101	('fuck', 'gay')	12
dick	0.894	99	('mentally', 'ill')	11
shut	0.560	62	('gay', 'ass')	10
suck	0.551	61	('ass', 'bitch')	10
fags	0.470	52	('eat', 'shit')	10
stupid	0.434	48	('shut', 'faggot')	9
kill	0.415	46	('ass', 'faggot')	9
hate	0.334	37	('gay', 'shit')	9
retarded	0.316	35	('fucking', 'gay')	9
tranny	0.316	35	('burn', 'hell')	8
pussy	0.307	34	('retarded', 'faggot')	7
queer	0.307	34	('fuck', 'fag')	7
dumb	0.289	32	('fuck', 'fucking')	7
die	0.289	32	('dick', 'die')	7
homosexual	0.271	30	('child', 'molester')	7
retard	0.271	30	('pussy', 'ass')	7
god	0.262	29	('shit', 'faggot')	7
ill	0.244	27	('fucking', 'bitch')	6
cunt	0.244	27	('bunch', 'faggots')	6
hell	0.235	26	('baby', 'raping')	6
disgusting	0.235	26	('fucking', 'faggots')	6
cock	0.235	26	('stupid', 'fucking')	6

Table 1: Top 30 most frequent words and strongest bigram associations in anti-LGBTQIA+ user-generated texts.

5.1 Analysis of Words in Anti-LGBTQIA+ User-generated Texts

To begin with, Table 1 and Figure 4 present the most frequently occurring words in anti-

Figure 4: Word cloud of top most frequent words of anti-LGBTQIA+ user-generated texts.

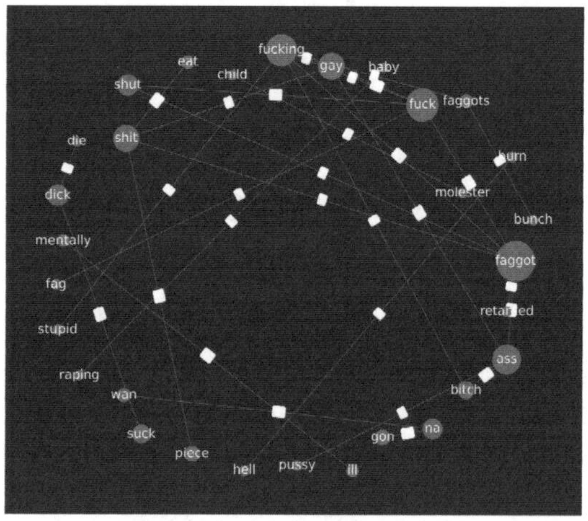

Figure 5: Bigram network graph of strongest associations between commonly occurring offensive contents of anti-LGBTQIA+ user-generated texts.

LGBTQIA+ user-generated texts (stop words removed), highlighting derogatory language and hate speech. The most common term, "faggot," accounts for 3.775% of occurrences (418 times), followed by profanity such as "fuck" (1.933%, 214 times) and "fucking" (1.852%, 205 times). Several slurs targeting LGBTQIA+ individuals, including "gay," "faggots," "fag," "tranny," and "queer," appear with notable frequency. Additionally, the presence of words associated with aggression (e.g., "kill," "hate," "die") and derogatory terms like "retarded" and "stupid" further underscores the negative sentiment in these texts.

Table 1 and Figure 5 present the top 30 strongest associations between commonly occurring offensive contents in anti-LGBTQIA+ user-generated texts. The most frequent bigram, "fucking faggot," appears 33 times, followed by other highly offensive phrases such as "suck dick" (24 times) and "fuck faggot" (23 times). Many bigrams include slurs targeting LGBTQIA+ individuals (e.g., "shut faggot," "gay shit," "retarded faggot") and general profanity combined with aggression (e.g., "burn hell," "dick die," "baby raping").

5.2 Model Performance

The results presented in Table 2 and Figure 3 highlight variations in performance among different LLMs in detecting anti-LGBTQIA+ user-generated texts. Notably, DeepSeek-V3 proves to be the best-performing model. It achieves the highest Acc and TPR of 0.866, along with the highest F1 of 0.871. Furthermore, it maintains the lowest FPR, indicating its high predictive performance in detecting anti-LGBTQIA+ user-generated text.

Next, Llama3.3-70B is the second-best method, achieving the highest Prec of 0.891, which underscores its effectiveness in minimizing false positives. It also shows notable high performance with Acc, TPR, F1, and FPR, which are just ranked below DeepSeek-V3.

Although the performance on all metrics remains comparatively lower than DeepSeek-V3 and Llama3.3-70B, GPT-4o-mini and GPT-4o have the best calibrated probabilistic predictions achieving the lowest $Brier$, with values of 0.551 and 0.585, respectively. Regarding GPT-o1-mini, it underperforms across all evaluation metrics compared to other LLMs, suggesting limitations in its effectiveness for the anti-LGBTQIA+ user-generated texts classification task.

Importantly, the $Brier$ values of all LLMs are notably high with all above 0.5, suggesting the necessity for improving probability calibration across them despite some delivering lower scores than others. Generally, LLMs exhibit overconfidence (Yu et al., 2024), as demonstrated by their calibration curves (Figure 3) falling below the 45° perfect calibration line (Bol et al., 2012). This suggests that the predicted probabilities (confidence score c as explained in Section 3.2) are higher than the actual likelihood of respective outcomes.

5.3 Error Analysis of Misclassified Texts

DeepSeek-V3 is proven to be the best-performing model in the previous section, but it still has limitations in accurately classifying anti-LGBTQIA+ user-generated texts. A closer examination of misclassified words reveals words that contribute to these errors (see Figures 6, 7, and Table 3).

High-frequency identity-related terms ("gay," "trans," "lesbian," "LGBT") frequently co-occur with neutral and offensive words, indicating the model's difficulty in distinguishing between discussions and harmful rhetoric. Additionally, offensive terms such as "fuck," "bitch," and "faggot" form toxic associations ("gay, shit"), underscoring the challenge of separating explicit hate speech from informal language. Furthermore, neutral words like "community," "gender," and "pride" appear in controversial contexts ("gay, community"), revealing limitations in contextual understanding.

These misclassifications highlight underlying sociocultural biases and detection limitations inherent within the model, with terms like "white," "straight," "god," and "fact" often reflecting ideological framing ("straight, white" and "gay, agenda"). Bigrams such as "fuck, stupid" and "gay, marriage" further highlight the model's struggle with contextual nuance, emphasising the need for improved context-aware learning to improve its performance.

Figure 6: Misclassified samples of anti-LGBTQIA+ user-generated texts from DeepSeek-V3 - Word cloud of top most frequent words.

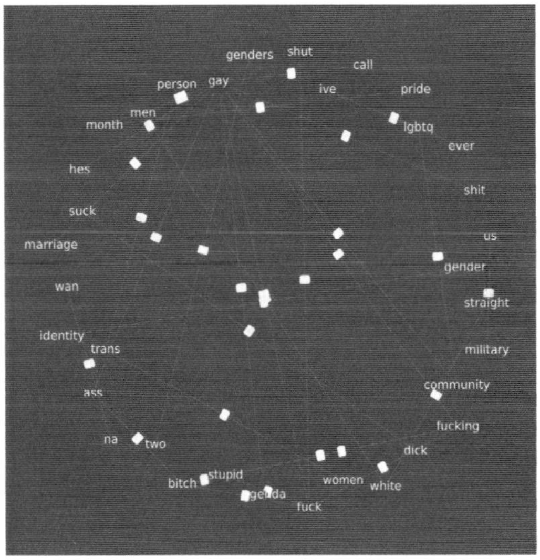

Figure 7: Misclassified samples of anti-LGBTQIA+ user-generated texts from DeepSeek-V3 - Bigram network graph of strongest associations.

Method	Accuracy ↑	TPR ↑	Precision ↑	F1 ↑	FPR ↓	Brier ↓
DeepSeek-V3 (Liu et al., 2024)	**0.866**	**0.866**	*0.890*	**0.871**	**0.160**	0.610
GPT-4o (Hurst et al., 2024)	0.820	0.820	0.878	0.828	0.242	*0.585*
GPT-4o-mini (Hurst et al., 2024)	0.838	0.838	0.880	0.844	0.208	**0.551**
GPT-o1-mini (Aaron et al., 2024)	0.769	0.769	0.832	0.779	0.283	0.610
Llama3.3-70B (Jonas et al., 2025)	*0.863*	*0.863*	**0.891**	*0.868*	*0.168*	0.634

Table 2: Performance comparison of different Large Language Models (LLMs) for detecting anti-LGBTQIA+ user-generated texts. **Bold value**: Best metric. *Italic value*: Second-best metric.

Word Frequency			Association Frequency	
Word	Percentage	Count	Association	Count
gay	3.473	224	('gay', 'men')	10
fuck	0.930	60	('gay', 'shit')	8
fucking	0.760	49	('ass', 'bitch')	6
trans	0.744	48	('fucking', 'bitch')	5
gays	0.713	46	('suck', 'dick')	5
bitch	0.651	42	('gay', 'community')	5
shit	0.589	38	('fuck', 'stupid')	5
women	0.496	32	('fucking', 'gay')	5
men	0.496	32	('two', 'genders')	4
dick	0.403	26	('bitch', 'fuck')	4
ass	0.372	24	('shut', 'fuck')	4
gender	0.372	24	('trans', 'person')	4
man	0.341	22	('gender', 'identity')	4
lesbian	0.326	21	('wan', 'na')	4
lgbt	0.310	20	('pride', 'month')	4
sex	0.310	20	('stupid', 'fucking')	4
community	0.310	20	('hes', 'gay')	4
faggot	0.310	20	('gay', 'ass')	4
suck	0.295	19	('gay', 'agenda')	4
person	0.279	18	('gay', 'fuck')	3
stupid	0.279	18	('fuck', 'fucking')	3
white	0.279	18	('trans', 'women')	3
straight	0.264	17	('stupid', 'bitch')	3
life	0.248	16	('straight', 'white')	3
pride	0.248	16	('lgbtq', 'community')	3
love	0.233	15	('white', 'men')	3
god	0.233	15	('us', 'military')	3
pussy	0.217	14	('call', 'gay')	3
lesbians	0.217	14	('ive', 'ever')	3
fact	0.217	14	('gay', 'marriage')	3

Table 3: Misclassified samples of anti-LGBTQIA+ user-generated texts from DeepSeek-V3 - Top 30 most frequent words and strongest bigram associations.

6 Conclusions and Discussions

This research proves the potential of LLMs for real-world applications in identifying anti-LGBTQIA+ user-generated content and underscores the valuable insights that text analysis can provide for topic modelling. These findings play a crucial role in fostering safer digital environments, ultimately improving protections for LGBTQIA+ individuals including their mental health and well-being.

To begin with, regarding the RQs outlined in Section 1, about **RQ1**, our analysis of anti-LGBTQIA+ user-generated texts (see Section 5.1) reveals a high prevalence of derogatory language, hate speech, and aggressive expressions. This can significantly contribute to topic modelling research. These findings underscore the urgent need for effective moderation strategies and improved detection models to mitigate harmful content and foster a safer online environment, improving the mental health and well-being of LGBTQIA+ individuals. Moreover, the proposed framework with the workflow in Section 3.2, including the developed prompt and experiments establish a general pipeline for leveraging LLMs in detecting anti-LGBTQIA+ user-generated texts, addressing **RQ2**.

For **RQ3**, as detailed in Section 5.2 while LLMs demonstrate promising performance in detecting anti-LGBTQIA+ user-generated texts, improvements are still necessary for real-world deployment. Firstly, performance varies across different metrics. DeepSeek-V3 and Llama3.3-70B emerge as the top-performing models; however, their calibration is not as good as GPT-4o and GPT-4o-mini. In contrast, GPT-o1-mini consistently underperforms across all metrics, underscoring its limitations in this task. Notably, despite achieving the highest performance, DeepSeek-V3 and Llama3.3-70B still fall short, with all key metrics (Acc, TPR, Prec, and F1) remaining below 0.9. This highlights the limitations of these LLMs in a zero-shot setting, emphasizing the need for fine-tuning and further development to enhance their reliability and applicability. On top of that, all LLMs exhibit **a notable calibration issue**, tending to be overconfident in their predictions. This overconfidence can lead to increased false positives and false negatives, resulting in unreliable moderation/classification of anti-LGBTQIA+ content. Additionally, it may amplify biases, reduce trust in AI-driven moderation systems, and create challenges in human-AI collaboration by insufficient moderators. Furthermore, as analysed in Section 5.3, although achieving the best-performing model, DeepSeek-V3 has limitations in distinguishing between neutral discussions and harmful rhetoric, struggles with contextual nuance, and exhibits sociocultural detecting limitations in detecting anti-LGBTQIA+ user-generated texts.

The findings of this study establish a strong foundation for future research. Future work should aim to enhance model performance through strategies such as few-shot prompting (Pengyue et al., 2024; Tom et al., 2020) which may significantly improve the predictive capabilities of LLMs in detecting anti-LGBTQIA+ user-generated texts. Additionally, utilising larger-scale datasets with different languages is a crucial next step. Additionally, ensuring demographic representation is critical for assessing LLMs' performance, and fairness across gender, nationality, LGBTQIA+ subgroups, and so on. These advancements will contribute to developing a robust, fair, and generalisable LLM-based anti-LGBTQIA+ user-generated text detection framework for protecting people of the LGBTQIA+ community.

References

Jaech Aaron et al. 2024. OpenAI o1 system card. *arXiv preprint arXiv:2412.16720*.

Roberto L Abreu and Maureen C Kenny. 2018. Cyberbullying and LGBTQ youth: A systematic literature review and recommendations for prevention and intervention. *Journal of Child & Adolescent Trauma*, 11:81–97.

Carolina Are, Catherine Talbot, and Pam Briggs. 2024. Social media affordances of LGBTQIA+ expression and community formation. *Convergence*, page 13548565241296628.

Adwita Arora, Aaryan Mattoo, Divya Chaudhary, Ian Gorton, and Bijendra Kumar. 2024. MEnTr@ LT-EDI-2024: Multilingual ensemble of transformer models for homophobia/transphobia detection. In *Proceedings of the Fourth Workshop on Language Technology for Equality, Diversity, Inclusion*, pages 259–264.

Bol, Linda, Hacker, and Douglas J. 2012. *Calibration*, pages 495–498. Springer US, Boston, MA.

Agostina Calabrese, Leonardo Neves, Neil Shah, Maarten W Bos, Björn Ross, Mirella Lapata, and Francesco Barbieri. 2024. Explainability and hate speech: Structured explanations make social media moderators faster. *Proceedings of the 62nd Annual Meeting of the Association for Computational Linguistics (Volume 1: Long Papers)*.

Waterschoot Cedric et al. 2022. Detecting minority arguments for mutual understanding: a moderation tool for the online climate change debate. In *Proceedings of the 29th International Conference on Computational Linguistics*, pages 6715–6725.

Han Chi et al. 2024. LM-Infinite: Zero-shot extreme length generalization for large language models. In *Proceedings of the 62nd Conference of the North American Chapter of the Association for Computational Linguistics: Human Language Technologies (Volume 1: Long Papers)*, pages 3991–4008.

Mirko Franco, Ombretta Gaggi, and Claudio E Palazzi. 2024. Integrating content moderation systems with large language models. *ACM Transactions on the Web*.

Gianluca Gini and Dorothy L Espelage. 2014. Peer victimization, cyberbullying, and suicide risk in children and adolescents. *Jama*, 312(5):545–546.

Robert Gorwa, Reuben Binns, and Christian Katzenbach. 2020. Algorithmic content moderation: Technical and political challenges in the automation of platform governance. *Big Data & Society*, 7(1):2053951719897945.

Aric Hagberg and Drew Conway. 2020. Networkx: Network analysis with Python. *URL: https://networkx. github. io*.

Steven A Hicks, Inga Strümke, Vajira Thambawita, Malek Hammou, Michael A Riegler, Pål Halvorsen, and Sravanthi Parasa. 2022. On evaluation metrics for medical applications of artificial intelligence. *Scientific reports*, 12(1):5979.

Melissa K Holt, Alana M Vivolo-Kantor, Joshua R Polanin, Kristin M Holland, Sarah DeGue, Jennifer L Matjasko, Misty Wolfe, and Gerald Reid. 2015. Bullying and suicidal ideation and behaviors: A meta-analysis. *Pediatrics*, 135(2):e496–e509.

Jun Sung Hong, Raúl Navarro, and Michelle F Wright. 2025. Adolescent cyberbullying: A worldwide concern. In *Encyclopedia of Information Science and Technology, Sixth Edition*, pages 1–22. IGI Global.

Danqing Hu, Bing Liu, Xiaofeng Zhu, Xudong Lu, and Nan Wu. 2024. Zero-shot information extraction from radiological reports using ChatGPT. *International Journal of Medical Informatics*, 183:105321.

Aaron Hurst, Adam Lerer, Adam P Goucher, Adam Perelman, Aditya Ramesh, Aidan Clark, AJ Ostrow, Akila Welihinda, Alan Hayes, Alec Radford, et al. 2024. Gpt-4o system card. *arXiv preprint arXiv:2410.21276*.

Cho Hyundong et al. 2024. Can language model moderators improve the health of online discourse? In *Proceedings of the 62nd Conference of the North American Chapter of the Association for Computational Linguistics: Human Language Technologies (Volume 1: Long Papers)*, pages 7471–7489.

Cascalheira Cory J et al. 2024. The LGBTQ+ minority stress on social media (missom) dataset: A labelled dataset for natural language processing and machine learning. In *Proceedings of the International AAAI Conference on Web and Social Media*, volume 18, pages 1888–1899.

Yuping Jin. 2017. Development of word cloud generator software based on python. *Procedia engineering*, 174:788–792.

Wihl Jonas et al. 2025. Data extraction from free-text stroke ct reports using GPT-4o and Llama-3.3-70B: The impact of annotation guidelines. *medRxiv*, pages 2025–01.

Taylor Jordan et al. 2024. Cruising Queer HCI on the DL: A Literature Review of LGBTQ+ People in HCI. In *Proceedings of the CHI Conference on Human Factors in Computing Systems*, pages 1–21.

Yubo Kou and Xinning Gui. 2020. Mediating community-AI interaction through situated explanation: the case of AI-Led moderation. *Proceedings of the ACM on Human-Computer Interaction*, 4(CSCW2):1–27.

Junlong Li, Jinyuan Wang, Zhuosheng Zhang, and Hai Zhao. 2024. Self-prompting large language models for zero-shot open-domain QA. In *Proceedings of the 62nd Conference of the North American Chapter of the Association for Computational Linguistics: Human Language Technologies (Volume 1: Long Papers)*, pages 296–310.

Aixin Liu, Bei Feng, Bing Xue, Bingxuan Wang, Bochao Wu, Chengda Lu, Chenggang Zhao, Chengqi Deng, Chenyu Zhang, Chong Ruan, et al. 2024. DeepSeek-V3 technical report. *arXiv preprint arXiv:2412.19437*.

Meta. 2025. Llama API platform. Accessed: 19 February 2025.

Falk Neele et al. 2024. Moderation in the wild: Investigating user-driven moderation in online discussions. In *Proceedings of the 18th Conference of the European Chapter of the Association for Computational Linguistics (Volume 1: Long Papers)*, pages 992–1013.

Joel Nothman, Hanmin Qin, and Roman Yurchak. 2018. Stop word lists in free open-source software packages. In *Proceedings of workshop for NLP open source software (NLP-OSS)*, pages 7–12.

L Haimson Oliver et al. 2021. Disproportionate removals and differing content moderation experiences for conservative, transgender, and black social media users: Marginalization and moderation gray areas. *Proceedings of the ACM on Human-Computer Interaction*, 5(CSCW2):1–35.

OpenAI. 2025. OpenAI API platform. Accessed: 19 February 2025.

Parth Patel. 2025. Detection of hate speech against lgbt+ on social media. Accessed: 2025-03-14.

Jia Pengyue et al. 2024. Mill: Mutual verification with large language models for zero-shot query expansion. In *Proceedings of the 62nd Conference of the North American Chapter of the Association for Computational Linguistics: Human Language Technologies (Volume 1: Long Papers)*, pages 2498–2518.

Sachdeva Pratik et al. 2022. The measuring hate speech corpus: Leveraging Rasch measurement theory for data perspectivism. In *Proceedings of the 1st Workshop on Perspectivist Approaches to NLP@ LREC2022*, pages 83–94.

Jha Prince et al. 2024. Memeguard: An LLM and VLM-based framework for advancing content moderation via meme intervention. *Proceedings of the 18th Conference of the European Chapter of the Association for Computational Linguistics (Volume 1: Long Papers)*.

O'Hagan Ross et al. 2023. The accuracy and appropriateness of ChatGPT responses on nonmelanoma skin cancer information using zero-shot chain of thought prompting. *JMIR dermatology*, 6:e49889.

Kaspar Rufibach. 2010. Use of brier score to assess binary predictions. *Journal of clinical epidemiology*, 63(8):938–939.

Masud Sarah et al. 2024. Hate personified: Investigating the role of LLMs in content moderation. In *Proceedings of the 2024 Conference on Empirical Methods in Natural Language Processing*, pages 15847–15863.

Ryan Schey and Stephanie Anne Shelton. 2023. Queer (ing) and trans (ing) critical media literacies in response to Anti-LGBTQIA+legislation and policies. *The International Journal of Critical Media Literacy*, 3(2):73–87.

Markov Todor et al. 2023. A holistic approach to undesired content detection in the real world. In *Proceedings of the AAAI Conference on Artificial Intelligence*, volume 37, pages 15009–15018.

Brown Tom et al. 2020. Language models are few-shot learners. In *Advances in Neural Information Processing Systems*, volume 33, pages 1877–1901. Curran Associates, Inc.

Raj Vivek et al. 2024. Conbert-rl: A policy-driven deep reinforcement learning based approach for detecting homophobia and transphobia in low-resource languages. *Natural Language Processing Journal*, 6:100040.

Qiao Wei et al. 2024. Scaling up llm reviews for google ads content moderation. In *Proceedings of the 17th ACM International Conference on Web Search and Data Mining*, pages 1174–1175.

Yuan Youliang et al. 2024. Does chatgpt know that it does not know? Evaluating the black-box calibration of ChatGPT. In *Proceedings of the 2024 Joint International Conference on Computational Linguistics, Language Resources and Evaluation (LREC-COLING 2024)*, pages 5191–5201.

Yuan Yu et al. 2024. Do llms overcome shortcut learning? an evaluation of shortcut challenges in large language models. In *Proceedings of the 2024 Conference on Empirical Methods in Natural Language Processing*, pages 12188–12200.

A Bayesian account of pronoun and neopronoun acquisition

Cassandra L. Jacobs
Department of Linguistics
State University of New York at Buffalo
Buffalo, NY, USA
cxjacobs@buffalo.edu

Morgan Grobol
MoDyCo
Université Paris Nanterre
Nanterre, France
lgrobol@parisnanterre.fr

Abstract

A major challenge to equity among members of queer communities is the use of one's chosen forms of reference, such as personal names or pronouns. Speakers often dismiss their misuses of pronouns as "unintentional", and claim that their errors reflect many decades of fossilized mainstream language use, as well as attitudes or expectations about the relationship between one's appearance and acceptable forms of reference. We argue for explicitly modeling individual differences in pronoun selection and present a probabilistic graphical modeling approach based on the nested Chinese Restaurant Franchise Process (nCRFP) (Ahmed et al., 2013) to account for flexible pronominal reference such as chosen names and neopronouns while moving beyond form-to-meaning mappings and without lexical co-occurrence statistics to learn referring expressions, as in contemporary language models. We show that such a model can account for variability in how quickly pronouns or names are integrated into symbolic knowledge and can empower computational systems to be both flexible and respectful of queer people with diverse gender expression.

1 Introduction

In contrast to words that are used to label referents as determined by convention (e.g., "cat" refers to CAT-like entities; Brennan and Clark, 1996), people have the autonomy to change their names and update their pronouns to reflect their identity (Zimman, 2019). In many Western cultures, however, personal names and pronouns are usually assigned *to* someone *by* others (e.g., one's parents or the norms of the ambient culture; Lind, 2023), and are highly conventionalized. For example, English canonically has only two animate third-person singular pronouns (i.e., he/him/his and she/her/hers). These pronominal forms as well as personal names are strong cues to gender identity. Within linguistics, this regularity has led to the general practice of treating referring expression generation as a form-to-meaning mapping problem (Enfield and Stivers, 2007). That said, the forms of reference used for someone are neither fixed, nor intrinsic properties of an individual. This paper presents a probabilistic modeling framework that respects a person's right to self-determination (of how to be referred to) without positing form-to-meaning or form-to-feature mappings. Our proposal accounts for the ongoing sociolinguistic change among young Westerners to ask and reinforce their understanding of their peers' self-identities.

The need for modeling pronoun and name use in natural language processing (NLP) is especially important given the increasing prominence of accommodating individuals' identities in the public sphere. Despite major advances in natural language generation, it has proven difficult to incorporate this into modern systems, especially in present-day neural network models. For example, even the most basic rule-based tokenization systems still do not flexibly handle nonbinary forms of address such as "Mx." Furthermore, large language models (LLMs) and commercial generative AI systems perpetuate bias against women and gender minorities by encoding harmful stereotypes in their training data (e.g., negative sentiment; Dev et al., 2021; Ungless et al., 2023) for in marginalized individuals' names, common professions, personal items, and pronouns. This is even more true for queer people outside the gender binary, as datasets regularly exclude nonbinary identities from their construction (Hall et al., 2023; Sakaguchi et al., 2021). Language that does not conform to gender stereotypes is also mishandled by NLP systems (Ghosh and Caliskan, 2023; Havens et al., 2022).

Here, we propose that systems that symbolically encode valid referring expressions for individuals are less prone to these problems. With present limitations in mind, we outline below the basic capabil-

Proceedings of the Queer in AI Workshop, pages 35–40
May 4, 2025

ities of an ideal system for learning the forms and representations of an individual's referring expressions such as names and pronouns must include:

1. Allow the introduction of new forms into the vocabulary (e.g., novel names or neopronouns)

2. Permit individuals to use a mixture of forms of reference for themselves (e.g., alternating between he/she/they or using different gendered forms in different languages; Moore et al., 2024)

3. Quickly adapt in the face of revision (e.g., updates to a person's name or pronouns), potentially given a single exemplar

4. Allow adaptation to vary by individuals

We further argue that such a system should produce more flexible adaptation for individuals who are more accustomed to such adaptation.

2 A Dirichlet process model of name and pronoun learning

Due to its symbolic nature, our proposed system can learn appropriate forms of address and reference through experience without encoding discriminatory knowledge such as an individual's appearance into their representations. This empowers queer people and supports their autonomy (Lind, 2023; Ovalle et al., 2023; Zimman, 2019). We treat the learning process as the assignment of probabilities of referential forms – pronominal or otherwise – directly to individuals rather than through the medium of individual characteristics (Lauscher et al., 2022).

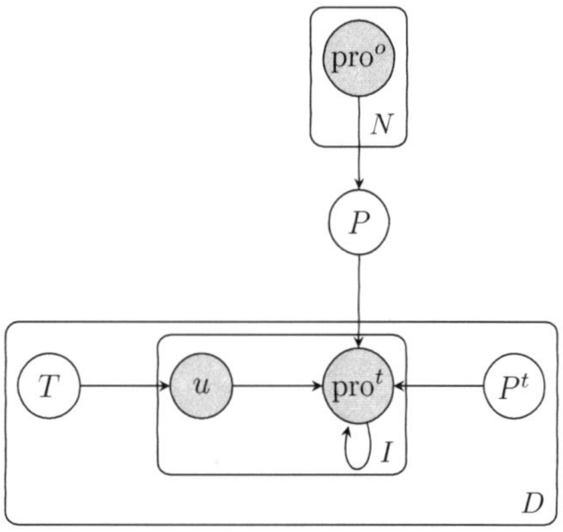

Figure 1: Single speaker model

Latent Dirichlet Allocation (LDA; Blei et al., 2001) is an algorithm that allows the probabilistic assignment of discrete labels (e.g., topics) to collections of events (e.g., documents) on the basis of the contents of the document (e.g., words). As suggested by the name, the topics learned by LDA are latent variables that are unobservable. In this modeling framework, documents are observable objects that are assumed to be generated by sampling words from mixtures of topics. Critically, a trained topic model can be used to estimate what proportion of topics was used to generate that document. These models are in principle infinite, and can have novel topics as well as additional vocabulary items added as a dimension in the vocabulary by trivial extension.

Building on this approach, the nested Chinese Restaurant Franchise Process (nCRFP; Ahmed et al., 2013) allows for models to even learn that different types of documents or users exist. For example, book chapters and magazine articles may have different lexical distributions, and authors within each of those genres may have different lexical preferences. Graphical models have been used to capture variation in language use across different geographical regions (Eisenstein et al., 2010) – analogous to the speaker communities of interest here. Simplified versions of Dirichlet processes (e.g., Beta-binomial priors) have also been applied to learning, as in learning and adaptation to syntactic structures in the context of a conversation (Kleinschmidt et al., 2012).

The present paper expands the metaphor of the nCRFP (Ahmed et al., 2013) to model an individual's learning of referring expressions – and specifically the pronouns – for others. We choose to treat pronouns or similar gender markers as observable objects that have probabilistic assignment to topics (communities of individuals), making pronouns most analogous to words in a document. Furthermore, we can characterize individuals or referents as "documents" that comprise a unique probability distribution over pronouns and names. Extending the metaphor to the hierarchical domain, different communities of learners (topics) may have priors of different strengths and/or more uniform expectations over pronoun use for unfamiliar individuals. Within topics, it is also clear that different groups of learners belong to different communities that reinforce the statistics of use of referring expressions within their communities.

3 Probabilistic graphical model of individual speaker preference

In Figure 1, we present the parametrization of the single-speaker model, which details how a speaker selects pronouns referring to a specific individual t across utterances as a function of their linguistic experience. This model involves the following variables (indices are omitted in the figure for brevity):

$\text{pro}^t_{d,i}$ Produced pronoun referring to t in the interaction i of discourse d. Can be absent, in case where the preferred pronouns are no pronouns. The self-loop allows for both pronoun stability and intentional alternation. That is, speakers can either select a chosen pronoun for a particular interaction, which they adhere to, or vary pronoun uses if the referent has indicated such a preference.

$u_{d,i}$ Utterance including a pronominal reference to t.

P The speaker's general prior on pronoun production.

P^t_d The speaker's prior on t's pronouns at the time of interaction d. The support of P^t_d is not necessarily pointwise, and its support and distribution are subject to adjustments between different interactions, for instance in case of offline feedback about a pronoun use.

T_d Topic for interaction d.

pro^o_n Pronoun usages witnessed by the speaker at all times and for any referent.

These variables are plated across the set D of all discourses (spoken or written) where the speaker has referred to t, the set I of all interactions in said discourse, and the set N of all interactions witnessed at all by the Speaker.

A Bayesian approach captures the intuition that some individuals may have more rigid "priors" over pronouns for specific speakers, and therefore choose to override the referent's choice of pronouns. While this relative stubbornness is expected among individuals who adhere to gender binaries, it could also arise in individuals who are willing to expand their pronominal inventory but struggle to do so without significant exposure to more diverse pronoun usages.

Note that our models do not assume any reliance on external characteristics. While we generally disagree with the practice, a speaker's prior belief over pronoun distribution could be jointly determined by both linguistic experience as well as the co-occurrence of such characteristics in order to account for intentional or unintentional misgendering.

4 Probabilistic graphical model of community norms

Speakers do not obtain their linguistic knowledge from pure distributional statistics. Rather, their preferences are contextualized by interactions with others in their language communities and through interactions with individuals that may reinforce those community beliefs. In cases where a speaker belongs to a community with practices that either accept and embrace — or deny — the practice of naming oneself (Lind, 2023), speaker priors are expected to be sampled from the community prior over pronouns as well.

For example, queer and cis-binary communities display clear differences in linguistic preferences and consensus about whether one's pronouns neatly correspond to one's current presentation suggests (Rose et al., 2023). This gives rise to the prediction that some speakers will not readily adapt to signals that (in a given conversation) the relevant pronouns to use belong to some set and not others (Arnold et al., 2024), particularly if their linguistic knowledge strictly excludes gender neutral or neopronouns. On the other hand, queer folks who have many friends whose pronouns fall outside the gender binary can be expected to have more flexible and more uniform beliefs about potential pronouns.

At the scale of a whole community, where pronoun usage witnessed by someone are those produced by other members of a the community, our model becomes that of Figure 2: for all triplets c, s, t of individuals in a community C, $\text{pro}^{s,t}$ is a pronoun used by a s to refer to t and $P^{c,t}$ and P^c are the priors of c about possible pronoun usages, respectively for t specifically, and for anyone. Note that the self-referring case $s = t$ is not excluded, and is in fact an important part in building priors for the rest of the community.

5 Related work

A challenge for modeling pronoun use in practical systems arises when we presuppose that learning words boils down to the problem of mapping form onto meaning. For instance, early connectionist ap-

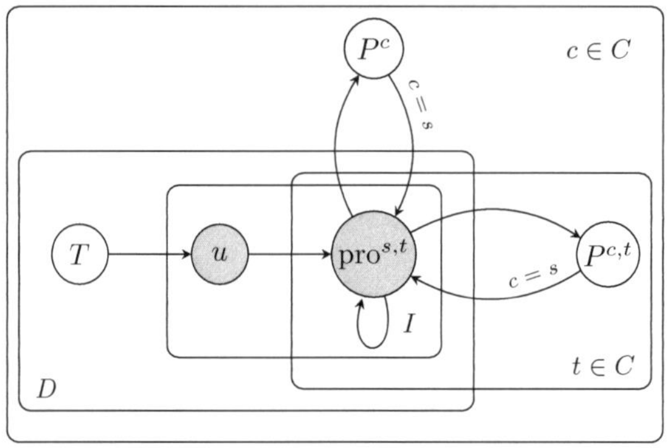

Figure 2: Community model with many speakers.

proaches to semantic representation, have treated the "meaning" of a word as a sparse d-dimensional vector consisting of several manually-selected semantic features (Cree et al., 2006; Rumelhart et al., 1986). Here, we propose that meaning be defined symbolically at the level of a referent rather than distributed across semantic features.

In word vectors trained on corpora, a "gender subspace" commonly emerges (Bolukbasi et al., 2016) that encodes social biases about canonical genders (e.g., stereotypes about the gender of nurses versus doctors). Pronouns and other high-frequency gendered nouns (e.g., man, woman) typically serve as critical anchors in the debiasing process, and serve as an excellent probe into the origins of biases in modern statistical NLP systems. Others have successfully demonstrated that non-binary pronoun LLM representations can be debiased, suggesting that the form-to-meaning mapping can be partially undone for novel referential forms (van Boven et al., 2024).

Being able to appropriately select the correct pronoun for a referent, as in text generation applications, is critical for ensuring equity and access to modern-day NLP tools. A number of studies have attempted to study gender bias in pronoun production. However, few of these studies have been able to probe the representations of pronouns, neopronouns, and name use that differs from the mainstream (Sakaguchi et al., 2021). The model we present here is capable of generating a wide variety of potential sentences to test the role of experience during fine-tuning of language models and thus improve gender inclusivity.

The present work is strongly informed by the integrative account presented in Ackerman (2019), who stated that cognitive, biological, and social factors combine to influence coreference resolution for non-binary people. They highlight that normatively unexpected mappings can nevertheless be made felicitous with sufficient supporting context.

6 Future Work

Our models allow for a straightforward integration of both witnessed pronoun uses and external priors in the process of pronoun selection in production. This provides a reasonably simple way to model pronoun acquisition during a long history of interactions in communities. However, for the sake of simplicity, certain interaction dynamics are not taken into account, and we leave to future work the search for improved models that balance the insights added by these refinements and the extra complexity that they would induce.

Our community model does not explicitly include non-linguistic social dynamics. Most importantly, language uses witnessed by a comprehender might have different weights depending on the speaker. For instance, the credit given to pronoun uses by speaker s for referent t could vary depending on how close to t s is assumed to be, and the $s = t$ case could be given a separate treatment. Furthermore, our models are only concerned with pronouns, which have the lightest semantic content of all referring expressions. However, it is likely that in practice, pronoun usage is also informed by the use of other referring expressions, such as names, formal titles, terms of address, etc. In our current model, these evidences are folded into the priors P, but more precise examination of their internal structure would provide a much richer model.

7 Conclusion

The model that we outline here shows that it is possible to represent individuals as possessing distributions of pronominal referring expressions, consistent with their own self-determined gender. The probabilistic graphical modeling accounts are flexible enough to allow learners to accommodate others based on their experience with linguistic variability in pronoun use. Additionally, the work provides a mechanism for the easy extension of one's linguistic vocabulary to incorporate novel pronouns, including but not limited to neopronouns, emojipronouns, and so on. We view this work as a critical bridge between cognitive scientific work on pronoun processing (Ackerman, 2019; Arnold et al., 2024; Rose et al., 2023) and computational modeling of linguistic variability (Eisenstein et al., 2010; Kleinschmidt et al., 2012) while also providing a way to advance equity in pronoun generation and comprehension (Ovalle et al., 2023; Piergentili et al., 2024; Lauscher et al., 2023).

References

Lauren Ackerman. 2019. Syntactic and cognitive issues in investigating gendered coreference. *Glossa: a journal of general linguistics*, 4(1).

Amr Ahmed, Liangjie Hong, and Alexander Smola. 2013. Nested chinese restaurant franchise process: Applications to user tracking and document modeling. In *International Conference on Machine Learning*, pages 1426–1434. PMLR.

Jennifer E Arnold, Ranjani Venkatesh, Zachary Vig, Jennifer E Arnold, Ranjani Venkatesh, and Zachary A Vig. 2024. Gender competition in the production of nonbinary 'they'. *Glossa Psycholinguistics*, 3(1).

David Blei, Andrew Ng, and Michael Jordan. 2001. Latent dirichlet allocation. In *Advances in Neural Information Processing Systems*, volume 14. MIT Press.

Tolga Bolukbasi, Kai-Wei Chang, James Y Zou, Venkatesh Saligrama, and Adam T Kalai. 2016. Man is to computer programmer as woman is to homemaker? debiasing word embeddings. In *Advances in Neural Information Processing Systems*, volume 29. Curran Associates, Inc.

Susan E Brennan and Herbert H Clark. 1996. Conceptual pacts and lexical choice in conversation. *Journal of experimental psychology: Learning, memory, and cognition*, 22(6):1482.

George S Cree, Chris McNorgan, and Ken McRae. 2006. Distinctive features hold a privileged status in the computation of word meaning: Implications for theories of semantic memory. *Journal of Experimental Psychology: Learning, Memory, and Cognition*, 32(4):643.

Sunipa Dev, Masoud Monajatipoor, Anaelia Ovalle, Arjun Subramonian, Jeff Phillips, and Kai-Wei Chang. 2021. Harms of gender exclusivity and challenges in non-binary representation in language technologies. In *Proceedings of the 2021 Conference on Empirical Methods in Natural Language Processing*, pages 1968–1994, Online and Punta Cana, Dominican Republic. Association for Computational Linguistics.

Jacob Eisenstein, Brendan O'Connor, Noah A. Smith, and Eric P. Xing. 2010. A Latent Variable Model for Geographic Lexical Variation. In *Proceedings of the 2010 Conference on Empirical Methods in Natural Language Processing*, pages 1277–1287, Cambridge, MA. Association for Computational Linguistics.

N.J. Enfield and T. Stivers. 2007. *Person Reference in Interaction: Linguistic, Cultural and Social Perspectives*. Language Culture and Cognition. Cambridge University Press.

Sourojit Ghosh and Aylin Caliskan. 2023. ChatGPT perpetuates gender bias in machine translation and ignores non-gendered pronouns: Findings across bengali and five other low-resource languages. In *Proceedings of the 2023 AAAI/ACM Conference on AI, Ethics, and Society*, AIES '23, page 901–912, New York, NY, USA. Association for Computing Machinery.

Siobhan Mackenzie Hall, Fernanda Gonçalves Abrantes, Hanwen Zhu, Grace Sodunke, Aleksandar Shtedritski, and Hannah Rose Kirk. 2023. Visogender: A dataset for benchmarking gender bias in image-text pronoun resolution. *Advances in Neural Information Processing Systems*, 36:63687–63723.

Lucy Havens, Melissa Terras, Benjamin Bach, and Beatrice Alex. 2022. Uncertainty and inclusivity in gender bias annotation: An annotation taxonomy and annotated datasets of British English text. In *Proceedings of the 4th Workshop on Gender Bias in Natural Language Processing (GeBNLP)*, pages 30–57, Seattle, Washington. Association for Computational Linguistics.

Dave F Kleinschmidt, Alex B Fine, and T Florian Jaeger. 2012. A belief-updating model of adaptation and cue combination in syntactic comprehension. In *Proceedings of the Annual Meeting of the Cognitive Science Society*, volume 34.

Anne Lauscher, Archie Crowley, and Dirk Hovy. 2022. Welcome to the modern world of pronouns: Identity-inclusive natural language processing beyond gender. In *Proceedings of the 29th International Conference on Computational Linguistics*, pages 1221–1232, Gyeongju, Republic of Korea. International Committee on Computational Linguistics.

Anne Lauscher, Debora Nozza, Ehm Miltersen, Archie Crowley, and Dirk Hovy. 2023. What about "em"? How Commercial Machine Translation Fails to Handle (Neo-)Pronouns. In *Proceedings of the 61st Annual Meeting of the Association for Computational Linguistics (Volume 1: Long Papers)*, pages 377–392, Toronto, Canada. Association for Computational Linguistics.

Miriam Lind. 2023. How to do gender with names: The name changes of trans individuals as performative speech acts. *Journal of Language and Sexuality*, 12(1):1–22.

Ashley R Moore, James Coda, Julia Donnelly Spiegelman, and Melisa Cahnmann-Taylor. 2024. Queer breaches and normative devices: language learners queering gender, sexuality, and the l2 classroom. *International Journal of Bilingual Education and Bilingualism*, 27(5):675–688.

Anaelia Ovalle, Palash Goyal, Jwala Dhamala, Zachary Jaggers, Kai-Wei Chang, Aram Galstyan, Richard Zemel, and Rahul Gupta. 2023. "i'm fully who i am": Towards centering transgender and non-binary voices to measure biases in open language generation. In *Proceedings of the 2023 ACM Conference on Fairness, Accountability, and Transparency*, FAccT '23, page 1246–1266, New York, NY, USA. Association for Computing Machinery.

Andrea Piergentili, Beatrice Savoldi, Matteo Negri, and Luisa Bentivogli. 2024. Enhancing gender-inclusive machine translation with neomorphemes and large language models. In *Proceedings of the 25th Annual Conference of the European Association for Machine Translation (Volume 1)*, pages 300–314, Sheffield, UK. European Association for Machine Translation (EAMT).

Ell Rose, Max Winig, Jasper Nash, Kyra Roepke, and Kirby Conrod. 2023. Variation in acceptability of neologistic English pronouns. *Proceedings of the Linguistic Society of America*, 8(1):5526.

David E. Rumelhart, James L. McClelland, and PDP Research Group. 1986. *Parallel Distributed Processing, Volume 1: Explorations in the Microstructure of Cognition: Foundations*. The MIT Press.

Keisuke Sakaguchi, Roland Le Bras, Chandra Bhagavatula, and Yejin Choi. 2021. WinoGrande: An Adversarial Winograd Schema Challenge at Scale. *Transactions of the Association for Computing Machinery*, 64(9):99–106.

Eddie Ungless, Bjorn Ross, and Anne Lauscher. 2023. Stereotypes and smut: The (mis)representation of non-cisgender identities by text-to-image models. In *Findings of the Association for Computational Linguistics: ACL 2023*, pages 7919–7942, Toronto, Canada. Association for Computational Linguistics.

Goya van Boven, Yupei Du, and Dong Nguyen. 2024. Transforming Dutch: Debiasing Dutch Coreference Resolution Systems for Non-binary Pronouns. In *Proceedings of the 2024 ACM Conference on Fairness, Accountability, and Transparency*, FAccT '24, pages 2470–2483, New York, NY, USA. Association for Computing Machinery.

Lal Zimman. 2019. Trans self-identification and the language of neoliberal selfhood: Agency, power, and the limits of monologic discourse. *International Journal of the Sociology of Language*, 2019(256):147–175.

Author Index

Association for Computational Linguistics
209 N. Eighth Street
Stroudsburg, Pennsylvania 18360

ISBN 979-8-3313-1927-4

9 798331 319274

CURRAN ASSOCIATES INC.
proceedings.com